To

John

Great to meet you

Bernie

YOUR SUCCESS IS:
Hidden
in
Your Daily Routine

by
Bernie De Souza

Published by
Global Training 4U,
Global Training House,
102a Warwick Street
Leamington Spa, UK
CV32 4QP

www.globaltraining4u.com

Cover design by
www.amoryhewson.co.uk

Illustrations by Raj Chohan
www.animatedrooms.co.uk

Photographs by Jaz Lall

ISBN-13: 978-0-9551928-1-4

Printed in Great Britain by:
J.H.Haynes & Co Ltd, Sparkford

ii

About the Author

Bernie De Souza has been a professional speaker for over twenty years. He is a sports coach, performance consultant, author and a playing member of the Marylebone Cricket Club (MCC). He has spoken extensively to large audiences in the UK and the USA, Europe and Australia.

Bernie first qualified as a physical training instructor in the Royal Air Force. Using his experience as a coach and trainer, he is able to provide insights into helping people and companies improve their performance and realise their potential. He has developed an international business through bringing out the best in people. His unique gift in mentoring and personal development has helped many to achieve their goals and dreams. His skill is to make business-building simple.

The information contained in this book will help those who are stuck to become unstuck and those who want to improve their performance to achieve new levels of success.

Foreword

In this book Bernie De Souza has drawn from his personal and business experience to highlight how the smallest changes in our lives can make huge differences.

It clearly and simply lays out how we can identify and implement changes in our lives that will help us all achieve more and be more. These are not some loose theories but tried and tested techniques that both Bernie and others have proven work in their lives to make real and profound changes.

We hope you will enjoy the book and take on board the information but most importantly, put it into action. We wish you every success in achieving your goals.

Allan & Barbara Pease
Best selling authors and motivational speakers
www.peasetraining.com

Dedication

To my sons
Luke and Josh
who are so special to me

This book is dedicated also to all those people who really want to do something to change their lives and move on beyond their present situation.

Acknowledgements

I am indebted to all the friends, near and far, who have helped me directly or indirectly, with their wise advice and encouragement to pursue this venture to completion. The excellent comments I have received have been a real inspiration. I am particularly grateful to my friend David Cook who has performed an incredible feat in translating my recordings into a readable form. His patience during our conversations has been truly remarkable.

Contents

Foreword..iv
Dedication and Acknowledgements.............................v
Preface...vii
Introduction..1

Day 1 Review - Early Days 8

Day 2 Opportunity – Starting point............................21

Day 3 Use **Goals** to a Destination 39

Day 4 Time with Coaches and Mentors.....................55

Day 5 Investigate - Your Responsibility 70

Day 6 Never, **Give Up** - Reset Your Goals...................84

Day 7 Evaluate - Summary......................................97

APPENDICES
A Seven Day Plan to Climb Your Mountain....................105
B Recommended reading..106
C Turbo-charge Your Performance..............................107

Preface

It is fair to say that 99% of people are 99% successful in one or more aspects of their lives. This book will help you to achieve that little extra performance that will allow you to move on in your chosen endeavour. There are observed differences in the daily routines of people who are considered successful compared to those who may be described as average. The factors which separate them have nothing to do with age, personality, intelligence, qualifications, gender, colour, or nationality.

After successfully coaching in companies and with individuals I have been encouraged to put this ROUTINE training formula in writing for the benefit of others. The principles and guidelines I share with you in this book are from my personal experience in spending time with many successful people in all walks of life. I have been enlightened by some priceless gems of wisdom from truly successful people.

Throughout this book I have endeavoured to keep the principles simple and relatable but, at the same time, to give you, the reader, guidelines on how to make progress in every area of your life. You may feel stuck and want to get unstuck to start moving again; or you may want to close the 'performance gap' between your present achievement level and your true potential. These principles can apply to your job, career, relationships, or any project you may undertake. From the evidence of our workshops I can guarantee that these guidelines will help you achieve any level of success you are prepared to work for.

Some books are read once and others read time and again. The principles included in this book are timeless yet the applications will grow and change to suit the user's needs. For instance, this book can also be used by parents in helping to raise their children. As my two sons grow I am encouraging them to develop their own daily routines which will help them; in school work, sports, leisure and social activities. My hope is that this will prepare and strengthen them to cope with different challenges in the future. Our daily routines have as much influence on our level of success as our children's routines have on theirs.

This book is written for people who may be quietly discontented about where they are in their lives and who may want to make a change. It may be young people just starting out in a career or embarking on a university course. You could be in a job that once challenged you but now has become monotonous and humdrum and you may want to take stock of where your life is taking you. On the other hand, you may just want to put some organisation into your busy hectic schedule.

It is said: "Knowledge is power and confidence". Alone it leads nowhere without dedication, commitment and application. About 10% of the working population make a serious effort to gain extra knowledge in their chosen field. Of this, only three apply the knowledge with passion and commitment. Just think, only 3% of the population actually make a conscious effort to be successful; yet so many more have the ability and opportunity.

Countless books have been written on the 'do's' and 'don't's', the 'how to' and 'how not to' develop a successful life. In the following pages you will find insights into the very subtle differences in daily behaviour patterns which determine whether a person is 'successful' or not. Some books are good for a season and others for a lifetime. Add your comments on the pages provided and you will find long lasting benefits as you establish your daily routine.

If you are looking for a magic solution or winning lottery numbers, I'm sorry to disappoint you. This book is about your daily routines; summarised in three words: Discover, Experience and Apply. This short book shows how a daily routine helped a young, disorganised man achieve success. By simply breaking down these tasks into daily, bite-sized routines, you can change your routine to achieve success. Start with a 7-day goal to complete reading this book.

After the Introduction, each 'Day', or chapter, should take between five and ten minutes to read. If you do not normally read as a habit, try to allocate a time in which you can read just one chapter each day so you develop a daily reading routine. Please take your time reading and answering the questions that follow honestly. After reading the chapter and answering go to Appendix A to begin or continue with the seven day climb of your mountain.

Bernie De Souza
October 2007

Your Success is Hidden in Your Daily

EVIEW

PPORTUNITY

SE GOALS

IME WITH MENTOR

NVESTIGATE

EVER GIVE UP

VALUATE

x

Introduction

If you are reading this book it's probably because you have that desire to move on from your present situation. The fact that you are reading it means you are what I call a 'mountain person'. Mountain people want to see the panoramic view; they are willing to make the effort to reach that one step further. They are prepared to go through challenging times. They may go hungry, thirsty, even tired, but they still make the effort; go that extra mile. They know that, by reaching their goal, the mountain-view is worth overcoming challenges and inconveniences. By reading a book like this you obviously want to learn more, take control of your life and change your future.

There are others I call 'valley' people; they are not prepared to stretch. They prefer to make excuses, live for the present. They are not really looking for the better views in life; they think those views are for others. They tend to do just enough and no more.

So it is a pleasure to write to 'mountain' people, because, with your attitude and this information, we can move on together.

Over the years I have been privileged to meet, interview, and associate with many successful people from different backgrounds. Their experiences, knowledge and insights reveal that there is a common essential feature in every successful person, irrespective of their profession.

It is their routine: what they do every day, through habit. You may have heard the expression: "The rich get richer and the poor get poorer." Why is this so? The answer is quite simple (and easy to learn). It's because of their daily routine. There's no magic in it. If you continue doing what you already do, you will continue getting the same results. There is no surprise in this; it's just an observable fact of life. Clearly, successful people have different attitudes, daily routines and reach different goals; they think differently from the rest.

Think about this: how many hours does a highly successful person have each day? How many hours does an average person have? The answer to both questions is the same: twenty-four. So really the difference between success and average is how we use our time. This book provides insights into how we can achieve more from our time so we can enjoy better results from our efforts. It's never too late to make that decision. Many people live their lives thinking that there must be more to life than what they are doing or have. Changes in the little things we do can result in huge differences to the outcomes.

The following pages are arranged based on a single acrostic: "ROUTINE". The subject for each day, or chapter, starts with a word beginning with a letter from ROUTINE. You may have been to the mountain or are now between the mountain and the valley. You now have an opportunity to return to the mountain top. By using ROUTINE anytime, you can get back on track up the mountain.

Remember - Your Success Is: Hidden in your daily ROUTINE.

In my training workshops I often set the scene by having the audience imagine two couples.

The first couple wake up naturally. He goes to the window, opens the curtain, and looks across the panoramic view of the lake in their immaculately landscaped grounds. He draws in a deep breath and, with an air of utter gratitude and pleasure he whispers: "Ah yes, a new day!"

They are living in their dream home. After completing their exercise routine the couple leisurely eat their meal in their breakfast room. (Imagine doing whatever you want each day)... They are excited about life and have planned their day, maybe shopping first then a river trip. Also they have planned some trips. They have a choice of cars in their spacious garage. The mail has arrived. It includes two first class tickets for an overseas holiday, one which they are invited to take.

For some people such a scene seems like a pipe dream or fantasy. "Is this really possible?" they ask.

The couple have come from ordinary backgrounds and achieved a lifestyle by working with a sense of purpose. They have simply decided to make things happen in their lives to benefit them and their family. They have established a daily routine that has brought them to this mountain-top place in their lives.

The second couple are also from ordinary backgrounds. However, they wake up to an infuriating alarm clock every morning, while it is still dark. "Oh no!" he mutters, "Another day!" He creeps around a much smaller house, careful not to disturb the rest of his family, puts on his socks hoping they are a matching pair. He has a quick shave, hoping he doesn't make a mess of his face. Time is pressing on and he hastily makes himself a coffee which he takes to drink in his car. With the coffee cup between his legs he dashes off to join the bumper-to-bumper queue. It is dark, miserable and horrible. He is on his way to a job that he may not like, to work for a boss and colleagues with whom he would rather not be.

These two couples live quite different lives. They both have choices. The first can live in the house of their choice and can choose their daily activities and when they take their vacations. The second couple does have choices but they are more limited based around his job.

When we take a serious look at the choices we make and change our daily routine, we can find that the end result is so much more beneficial to us and everyone around us.

The difference in the two couples' day is the result of established life patterns, not instantly, as with winning the lottery or football pools, but rather over a period of months and years.

Every day we make choices and decisions. We are where we are at any given moment as a result of the choices and decisions we have made along the way from childhood.

The choices we make are a reflection of our values and what is important to us.

A significant factor separates the two couples. The first know and agree **WHAT** they want in their lives; they know **WHY** they want it and have a system and a daily routine, including **HOW** they intend to achieve it. They are prepared to work effectively for it, with enthusiasm, to achieve their goals.

How do I know this is possible? I and many of my close friends and associates have been in the situations of both couples. It was a dedication to the principles in this book that led me to develop ROUTINE and as a result I moved from the second lifestyle to the first. I've successfully helped others do the same.

You may have already achieved some of your goals – a nice house, car, holidays, etc. Could you guarantee maintaining your lifestyle in later years? When everything is paid off, and you look at your net worth, will you be shocked? And are you working to satisfy and meet your own goals or someone else's?

I will share my story and how my life changed by asking and answering honestly two simple questions. First: Is this how I want my life to be? Second: Are you being paid what you are worth, or what your job is worth? Think about this; Is your quality of life suffering because of your job? A recent survey in the United Kingdom and Ireland showed that, on average, people worked longer hours than anywhere else in Europe. Currently, as a nation, we enjoy less free time and disposable income than ever before. Thankfully you can change the outcome. Let's look at your daily routine.

Key lesson

It is important to learn the power of questions particularly self-enhancing questions. At the end of each chapter are some questions you may wish to ask yourself. Add your own to the lists.

1   *Am I where I would like to be in life?*

2   *What do I really want in my life?*

3   *Will my present work help me to achieve it?*

4   *Do I have a daily routine?*

5   *What changes could I or should I make in my daily routine?*

6   *How do I expect this book to help me?*

 **WHAT I HAVE LEARNT TODAY**

REVIEW

Day 1

REVIEW - Early Days

"Train up a child in the way he should go: and when he is old, he will not depart from it"   *Proverbs 22:6*

Today's subject is **REVIEW**. Each day, week, month and year we need to review what we have done; what we have achieved. In this chapter I have reviewed my own life. I realise that, if my past determined my future, I would not be where I am today. It's not where you come from that's important but where you are going.

Think back to your childhood and youth. Think of some of your past successes in life; learning to ride a bike, learning to swim, learning to play a musical instrument, or subjects at school that you were good at and exams you passed. You will probably find that all your successes were the result of practice and also that you enjoyed what you were doing. Can you remember your dreams and ambitions during your school years? Have you fulfilled them? Have they changed as a result of life experiences?

When I think back over my life one thing I have aimed to do is to work more efficiently and by making better use of my time, I have found it helpful to categorise tasks under four headings beginning with "D":

(1) DO IT - do only those tasks that only you can do or that you know you do best. This creates so much time.

(2) DATE IT IN DIARY – events that you have to deal with in the future such as dates of training meetings, meeting rooms etc, so you don't have to put any mental energy into these things, all you have to do is to put dates on them.

(3) DELEGATE IT – when you accept that you cannot do everything you can delegate tasks and activities which are outside your range of skills, your life becomes a lot easier, especially if other people can do them more effectively than you. Some people try to do too much or are afraid to delegate. If you are one of those you need to "get over yourself and get going." You may tell yourself you are still a good boss, manager or whatever. You are not shirking your responsibilities but making team relationships stronger by delegating or sharing some of the work. You can say that you are smart to have found such an efficient way to get more done.

(4) DUMP IT - many things you can dump. We carry so much that we don't need. We worry about things that are not going to happen. Why do we do that? Really I am not sure at all. Dumping things clears your mind and helps to keep you focussed on working your plan for the future.

I am the eldest of four children: two boys and two girls. My dad was an engineer in the Royal Air Force, and as a result, we lived wherever he was based. My earliest memories are of living in Singapore. I was under three years old. These memories include riding a tricycle and seeing alligators - I don't know why but they looked like monsters to me. From Singapore we moved back to the UK, first to Swindon and then Royal Air Force Lyneham before my dad retired from the Service.

I was eight when we moved to Calne in Wiltshire, to an estate that was a mixture of council and private houses. I went to a local Catholic school, St Edmund's. It was very small and not very well structured for sport, a subject which I enjoyed. To make up the numbers for the teams two teaching age years had sports lessons together. I used to hang out with the older boys and, through sport, they accepted me. As a result, I very soon joined the school football team. I first played football for the school when I was eight years old. The others in the team were around ten. As well as sports I also learnt to play chess and became school chess champion.

I moved to the John Bentley Comprehensive School aged eleven. I was intellectually able and yet disliked school, particularly the academic subjects. I loved sport because it gave me recognition with my peers. I was very competitive and wanted to succeed. Through the training and encouragement of my P.E. teacher, Mr John Spencer, I became captain of the school cricket and football teams.

Mr Spencer was the assistant coach for the Wiltshire under 15s cricket team and it was through him that I was introduced to Mr Alan Crouch, the senior coach. Through these two gentlemen I was given my first breakthrough opportunity to play cricket for Wiltshire against Gloucestershire at Cheltenham College. It was a real eye opener for me. The team arrived at this very prestigious private boarding school, over 150 years old, set in elegant grounds and having magnificent buildings.

There were a lot of spectators at the game and all the players were very nervous. I only just scraped into the team. The Gloucestershire side had a tall, black West Indian guy called David Lawrence. His nickname was Sid Lawrence. He looked about ten years older than the rest of us, with a huge physique looking down on everyone in both teams. At that time he was arguably the fastest bowler in the UK for his age. All the batsmen in our team were terrified of him.

Mr Crouch really inspired me with his team talk before the match. With his words ringing in my mind I was afraid of nothing when I went out to bat. I felt that I could do anything. What I may have lacked in technique, I made up for in courage. I went on to make the highest score in the game, winning the match for Wiltshire and scoring my first 50.

Sid Lawrence later went on to play for England.

Whilst I was still at school, I played football for Calne Town Football Club. It was great to be paid to play football. It was something I really loved doing and it earned me more money than my newspaper round. My life centred on sport. The only reading I did outside school was in the sports pages at the back of the newspaper.

Think back – what are your happy memories of achievement? Did you ever keep a diary? If you didn't then one change you could make is to keep a journal. That way you could keep track of all your questions and progress in one location. Some people use a PDA or cell phone for on-the-spot records.

I remember one occasion as if it were yesterday. My dad had promised me a football strip if I passed a particular mathematics test at school. I was motivated by the thought of having my own football strip. In just one week he taught me the multiplication tables. He encouraged me every day as we practised them together. I repeated them over and over until I knew them by heart. I enjoyed the process because I was spending time with my dad and I had a reason to succeed; to have my own football strip. For me that was a goal. I really worked hard that week and easily passed the test. In fact, I had answered all the questions correctly, not just some or most. Suddenly, in one week, I had moved from the bottom group in the class to the top. I had the highest score for the test.

If you set your mind to something you can achieve it.

The teachers were very suspicious of my result and were convinced I had cheated. They made me do another, different test, on my own. Again, my marks were very high. I had succeeded in one of my worst subjects - but no football strip was forthcoming. My mum gave my dad such a hard time that, two weeks later, he gave me something even better - an England track suit. It cost him a lot more than the strip would ever have cost.

I learnt two important lessons from that exercise. I have endeavoured to apply them in my own life, particularly with my children and work associates.

1   *If you promise to do something do it on time; otherwise you lose credibility with the person to whom you gave the promise. Do what you say you will do; let your "yes" be "yes" and your "no" be "no".*

2   *If something has to be done that you don't like doing, work at it as best you can until it's done.*

My parents separated when I was fourteen. It is easy to look back in life and blame your circumstances or background and to make excuses that you didn't have a good start in life, or why you're not where you would like to be. One thing was certain for me. I knew I wanted to make money somehow. At that age I didn't understand the value of money but I knew I wanted to be better off. I had no idea how to start and no clear plan to achieve this ambition. My burning desire was to progress beyond my situation at that time. I was determined that nothing should stop me in this search.

If you want to do something, you'll find a way.

If you don't want to do something, you'll find an excuse.

Think about this if you decide to find an excuse make sure it is a good one because you'll have to live with it for the rest of your life!

After my parents split up my mum brought up the four of us up as a single parent in a council house. She had more than one job to make ends meet. The local swimming pool was a highlight for us each month. On one occasion we couldn't afford to go swimming that day. Naturally, I was disappointed, and also sensed my younger brother and sisters' sadness. In that moment, I said to myself: "I'm never going to let my children be disappointed like this. When I sort myself out and get a job or a career or even a business, I'll make sure we have our own swimming pool." In defining moments like these we make lasting decisions for our lives.

One of the benefits I have had from building my businesses is that we have been able to have our own swimming pool. Sometimes, your reviewing such events helps you determine what you really want for your future.

Another childhood memory is of us, a family of five, sharing a combined toilet and bathroom in the house. If you know what that is like, or can imagine three females and two males in a house sharing one bathroom, you know that the guys don't always get first choice. So another lasting decision I made for my own life was to always have more bathrooms than people living in the house. That way everyone is assured of a bath or shower whenever they want one. Little things like that, when you're young, can influence your thinking. You can either become more determined to achieve something or you can just accept life the way it is. It's a choice - your choice.

It is the strength of your determination that will affect whether or not you accept that life is the way it is.

Once, on my way to play in a match for Calne Town Football Club, my neighbour's house was on fire and they were panicking. Their concern was for a baby in a top floor bedroom. Being a council estate the houses were identical. I knew how to climb into my own bedroom because I had been locked out quite frequently in the past and this was my regular way into my own house. There was smoke everywhere. I think the local newspaper report gave me more credit for saving the girl than I really deserved. It would be nice to think this was a modern day hero in action but, in this instance, the neighbours benefited from my daily routine of losing or forgetting my house key.

After the match we went for a few beers and I was drunk on just two pints. From there I went to a rather lively party. Somehow I leaned against a window and cracked it. The point of including this story is to say that, I was remembered more in the neighbourhood for the cracked window than my rescue of the baby from the fire.

You find in life that negative events or actions tend to be remembered by other people far longer than positive ones.

Successful people learn from their mistakes and do not dwell on them.

Although I was very good at sports I left school at sixteen with no academic qualifications. I applied to do a four-year apprenticeship in a small engineering company. On my first day I walked into the workshop and felt how drab and depressing the work benches and environment were. It dawned on me that this was not what I wanted for a lifelong career. One employee had worked there for twenty-five years. I asked him if he enjoyed the work. "What do *you* think?" he bellowed. I walked out that day giving up an opportunity to learn a technical trade.

I had to get a job somehow. This was the only way I knew to earn a living. I asked myself: "What do I like doing most?" The only answer for me was something to do with sport. I decided to join a two-year, full-time sports course at the local college. At the college I met a girl who, to me, stood out from the rest; she later became my wife.

During the course, to earn some money, I took an evening job cleaning at the engineering company I had earlier rejected for the apprenticeship. After the sports course I applied to the Royal

14

Air Force for entry to train as a Physical Training Instructor. At the time there was a waiting list of five thousand applicants for fifteen places. None of those places was for me.

After missing out on the selection by the Royal Air Force I had to find a job, just any job for some wages. I didn't give up on the idea of becoming a Royal Air Force PTI one day. I knew that another opportunity would come round again and I held on to the vision of me as a sports teacher or coach, playing in the Royal Air Force teams and travelling the world. During this time a Royal Air Force PTI, Rudy Farquharson, encouraged me and answered my questions. Rudy had left my school three years earlier and was already where I was heading. He helped me prepare for the military life.

Successful people find mentors to help them achieve.

After leaving college I tried various jobs; the first was a temporary job in an egg factory. I wouldn't recommend this to anyone unless that's what they really want to do. No matter how often I washed and bathed I still smelled of eggs. To me it wasn't the greatest job in the world. I resented my predicament and felt that after spending twelve years at school, surely there must be more to life than this routine. Was this what life was about? Surely, this work could not possibly get me my dreams.

I saw no future in my work but I was persistent and determined to do something with my life. So, aged nineteen, I succeeded, on my second attempt, in joining the Royal Air Force.

One day, in the staff canteen, I shared my dream with my work colleagues. They had just been moaning about their situation. I said: "Well, the good news is that I have been accepted into the Royal Air Force. Very soon, I shall start a completely new way of life with an opportunity to make a career in sport, meet people and travel the world. I love sports and travel, so it's great for me."

At that time these 'friends' were my 'work-mates'. They asked me: "What do you want to do that for?" I replied: "To progress my life and have a career." Then they thought of all sorts of negative reasons why I should stay, saying: "Well you could get posted at short notice; you could get bosses you don't like; you might have to go to war, you might have to do things you don't want to do. Just think of the discipline in the forces. We wouldn't advise you to do that. Stay with us, it's safe here; it's easy. The pay is good and we get paid every week. We know where we're going, we come in every day, we're your friends, think about it, why take the risk outside?" The lesson here is that everyone wants you to get ahead, just not ahead of them.

Successful people define their own dream and pursue it.

Review your day and read out loud to yourself your goals and dreams twice daily, when you get up in the morning and when you go to bed at night. Doing this one activity alone puts you with the top earners in the country.

The Curious Frog

A tadpole hatched out at the bottom of a well. He was very happy living in the well as he grew into a frog. There was enough in the well to keep him occupied and well fed.

One day he was aware of the daylight at the top of the well shaft. He wondered what it must be like up there so he climbed up to see what was at the top.

To his amazement he saw a pond, so much bigger than his well. He thought: "This is great. It's much better than back home in the well." He settled in the pond for a time before he wanted to travel further. This time he found a lake, even bigger than the pond. He gasped at the sight. "Surely this must be the biggest expanse of water there can be."

Later he decided to travel again and eventually he arrived at the ocean. All he could see was water.

He realised how limited his thinking had been in the past.

Key lesson

Consider the skills you have.

1   What am I good at?

2   Do I enjoy doing that?

3   Could it lead me to a career?

4   What am I weak at?

5   Could that weakness be strengthened by practice?

6   Do I mix with people who are helpful in life?

7   Do they help or hinder me to achieve my life goals?

# WHAT I HAVE LEARNT TODAY

OPPORTUNITY

Day 2

Opportunity - Starting Point

"Twenty years from now you'll be more disappointed by the things you didn't do than by the ones you did."   Mark Twain

"Our philosophy of life is not best expressed in words but in the choices we make. In the long run we shape our lives and we shape ourselves. The choices we make are ultimately our responsibility."   Eleanor Roosevelt

Today the subject is **OPPORTUNITY**. This is the starting point for a change in your life. Opportunities come and go. When you are prepared for one you will take it. If you are not prepared you may not even notice it, or you may simply see it as hard work.

The person who looks for opportunities as part of his daily routine more often than not will find them.

You may think you haven't started on the '*road to success*'. You may be looking desperately to change some things in your life. You may feel that there is more to life than you have done or are doing right now. This is the time when you will find it very helpful to have a better understanding of yourself, your personality and how you behave in different situations.

One of the greatest lessons that I've learned is about myself because once I understood myself I was better able to

21

recognize good opportunities for me and to take full advantage of them. Previously I might have thought something was a GREAT opportunity however, due to my personality or some other reason the opportunity and I didn't seem to fit.

Things dramatically changed for me in 1994. I had an opportunity to learn about human behaviour and personality styles. Dr Robert Rohm, the founder of Personality Insights Inc., and I had been invited to a conference in America as guest speakers. This one event was the starting point to a big change in my life. I am personally indebted to Dr Rohm for introducing me to the D.I.S.C. method of personality assessment of the four drives in human behaviour.

I attended one of his sessions and was amazed at his one hour presentation. He spoke with authority, enthusiasm and great wit. He outlined the four basic drives that determine people's behaviour patterns.

Some people are outgoing while others are reserved; some are people-oriented while others are task-oriented. These are described by a language using the letters "D.I.S.C"; "D" for the Dominant, Outgoing type; "I" for the Inspiring, Outgoing type; "S" for the Supportive, Reserved type; and "C" for the Cautious, Reserved type. Our personalities are a blend of all four of these drives. Our blend, or personality style, is assessed through our answers to a series of questions about our behaviour in different situations. The assessment is not judgmental; it does not say our answers are right or wrong.

After the session I spent some time with Dr Rohm in the VIP lounge. We covered personalities in more depth. He did my profile and I was quite amazed at how accurate it was. The more I found out about myself the more fascinated I became in this assessment method.

I have since been to the USA and taken several courses to learn as much as possible about this aspect of human behaviour.

Understanding this subject is very powerful and has helped me in my personal life and work. Like a light being switched on, I can now see so much more clearly and understand why people do the things they do and the way they do them. People do not do things just to annoy you. It's the way they are 'wired'.

Dr Rohm puts it this way:

"People do not do things against you, they do things for themselves."

My personality profile highlighted areas in my life that needed to be addressed. The presentation was so positive that I wanted to address them. If I had had such insight and understood myself when I was much younger, the results of my work would have been quite different. I would have seen things differently. I am now more aware of why I do things and how I can achieve better outcomes from my choices and actions.

Knowledge of our personality style is so important for relationships and communication; from school right through into adult life. This includes our career, marriage and leisure interests. Studies show that the major reason people leave their jobs or lose them is not through technical incompetence but relational incompetence. First we need a better understanding of ourselves then we can understand another person through their personality style. Creating better relationships is then achieved through adapting our personality style.

Since my training and accreditation in this field I have run workshops for companies, colleges and families. If you would like to know more about your personality style I recommend a good starting point would be to visit our web site: www.globaltraining4u.com or come to one of our workshops where you can get to know yourself better through your personality style. This will also help you to understand and get on with others a lot better.

You don't have a second chance to make a first impression.

Wherever you are in life is the sum total of all that you have done and the choices you have made. Your past is history. You cannot change it. It does not help by dwelling on it. But, you can learn from it.

Some time ago I had an opportunity to meet and work with Vinod Kambli. In his youth he had been a bright and promising young cricketer. He made his debut for India in the late 1980's. He was dashing, exciting, flamboyant and he had the attention of everyone around the world in the cricketing fraternity.

He equalled the record set by Sir Donald Bradman of two double-centuries and a century in a row. Even when aged 24, he was dropped by India his innings averaged over 50 in test cricket.

This extremely talented young cricketer had, as his best friend from school, Sachin Tendulkar, an Indian cricketing legend. These boys hold the record for an innings together; scoring almost 700 runs between them for their school. Sachin has since become a legend in cricket and Vinod, even though he has a great career as a media expert eye commentator, never fulfilled his cricketing potential. I believe this was because the team management at that time did not fully understand him. In his younger days his performance was far more prominent than Sachin's. He now holds all the records for test runs and one-day international runs. I believe the Indian team management really had no idea how to deal with superstars or different personality types.

Having coached players, stars, workers and bright students at school, I can see how people are mismanaged simply because their seniors don't really understand personalities and human behaviour. Vinod's personality is very influential and inspiring, out-going and great with people. His behaviour confused the Indian team hierarchy into thinking that he only wanted the limelight. They thought his presence was destructive to the team.

Being a party type of person, loved by the crowd, didn't help him with a strong minded Indian coach. At that time the players were unable to make corrections themselves and it was a tragic shame that the cricket world should lose Vinod Kambli's ability and charisma.

Ten years ago I was working with Vinod in Mumbai. I've also had the privilege of working with him on other projects. When I did his personality profile for him it became quite obvious because he was both dominant and inspiring. He felt the need to express himself, to entertain and give people so much pleasure. Since his departure from cricket he has excelled in other arenas. He has taken advantage of many opportunities in acting and media work.

Your vision of your future is the picture you hold in your mind of whatever you desire or expect in life. This is all-important and is your motivation for all that you do whether consciously or unconsciously. All the decisions and actions in your daily routine are directed towards the fulfilment of this vision. The clearer the vision you have, the more disciplined your efforts will be to turn that vision into reality and the more likely you are to recognise the right opportunities when they come your way. Your passion, purpose, and power will all work together with your determination.

Successful people spend time focussing on their goal.

Your daily routine should include time to think about your vision and develop it clearly in your mind's eye.

During my Royal Air Force service a friend suggested I look at a business opportunity that I could start part-time. It was just before Christmas. I was hard up and in debt. The proposition seemed very attractive to me so I agreed to attend a training conference with him. It was there that I was able to see the bigger picture of the business and where it could take me if I followed the training pattern suggested.

I saw the business as an opportunity for my personal freedom and I didn't know that I was even looking for it. However I took the opportunity and through hard work achieved my dream of personal freedom.

Even though I didn't understand all the aspects of the work, I registered and began with enthusiasm. The training programme included reading books and listening to training CDs. I followed the system for six months, yet my business did not grow. I was dismayed, dejected and discouraged and wondered what was going wrong. Yet I knew I was developing 'internally'. My attitudes and habits were changing; I was beginning to learn that the key to success in my life was within me. If my effort was going to bear fruit then it was up to me and my actions to make it happen. My mentor at that time lived at a distance so I couldn't expect him to be there to help me all the time. I didn't have a phone, and there were no mobiles in those days. So my contact with him, and anybody else, was through the public phone box down the road. The training had changed my attitude. Instead of giving up I determined to succeed.

Initially, I was reluctant to create a clear picture of what would motivate me. An associate then asked me to go with him to look at houses; something he thought would spur him into action in his own business. As we looked at the houses, one seemed to feel just right for me. I could not afford it then but it became a personal goal. The clear vision of having that house made me work more effectively in my business. By staying focussed I got more done in every 24 hours. So after a few months I was able to buy the house.

At a conference in America I met one couple who have since had a major influence in my life. Dr Peter and Eva Muller-Meerkatz have a vibrant energy and zest for life. Meeting Peter and Eva was an opportunity that has helped me reach heights in my life that were just fantasy, now they are reality.

One year Peter and Eva had a desire to go to Hawaii, to Honolulu and the beaches. They invited me to go with them. The condition was that I would run the Honolulu Marathon with them. I had never run a marathon. Suddenly I had a goal to go to Hawaii. My attitude towards marathons changed; to run in such idyllic conditions would be an exhilarating new challenge. Spending time with Peter and Eva, and learning from their experiences of building global businesses would be priceless.

My starting point for this 'expedition' was to prepare for the marathon; you don't just wake up one morning and say: "I'll run a marathon today." I needed to be physically fit, at least fit enough to complete the run in a hotter climate. I worked out how many months I had and how much training I could do each month. When you're faced with dark mornings, wind and rain blowing round the corners there are times when you want to turn over in bed and have another hour's sleep. But my vision of being there with 25,000 other runners, in such a beautiful climate, spending time with Peter and Eva and the possibility of being a "finisher" was powerful enough to let me overcome short term pain and discomfort.

We all develop a vision of what we would like in our future. Successful people focus on this vision each day. They make it a daily routine to think about their vision. It may seem uncomfortable at first. When it becomes a habit, it will seem natural to you.

The Honolulu Marathon is a prestigious world class sporting event, for me, out of this world. It has been going since 1973 (when there were only 167 runners).

It was 5.00 a.m. The sky was dark, the pleasant trade wind wafted in from across the Pacific Ocean. The cannon fired, and we were on our way from the Ala Moana Boulevard in Honolulu running in a westerly direction towards the business area of the city with skyscrapers all around. Then, suddenly, the sky was lit up, brilliant, with a fantastic firework display. After downtown

27

Honolulu we headed upwards to the Diamond Head, a hill 230 metres high, created by a volcanic eruption millions of years ago. As we ran in the dark I became aware of the beautiful fragrance of the tropical flowers which were around me either side along the way; something awesome to remember.

The course leads in a south-easterly direction towards the coast, where the first glimmer of daybreak could be seen on the horizon across the ocean. Slowly but surely a spectacular sunrise emerged, emblazoned in the sky above the ocean. For me, tiredness and 'pain barriers' all melted away at such a magnificent sight. Many of the runners had cameras with them so they could take their own personal photos as memories of the fantastic views and scenery. We ran back up to Diamond Head again and then down the long slope to the finish line in the Kapiolanl Park in Waikiki. We were given a sea-shell necklace and sent to the Finisher's tent. We were presented with our t-shirt with 'I'm a Finisher' on the back. We also received a medal.

For the remaining days of our stay we were given VIP treatment wherever we went wearing the Finisher's t-shirt. In all the coffee bars and restaurants people allowed us to go to the front of the queue. The t-shirt was instant recognition and credibility.

It was a tremendous experience for me to have the opportunity to spend time in Honolulu, Hawaii. Could this be one of your dreams?

The key to pursuing an opportunity to the fullest is keeping the motivation as high as possible. As I look back I'm thankful that my dream of being involved in sport in the Royal Air Force was greater than the 'obstacles' my work colleagues or 'friends' tried to put in my way. The more I found out about becoming a PTI in the services the stronger it became my burning ambition. I followed my dream and jumped at the opportunity. That discipline and training paid off years later to help me complete the marathon.

The dream was big enough to give me the determination to ignore my friends and overcome the challenges that could have held me back.

If your burning desire is to change your circumstances, the people you mix with and what you earn, then association is a key factor in your daily routine. A major influence on your thinking will come from the books and papers you read, the TV programmes and DVDs you watch, the audio tapes and CDs you listen to daily and the people you associate with. By taking the opportunity to feed your mind with positive, inspirational, worthwhile knowledge and thoughts you invest in yourself and your future.

Just imagine loving parents helping their children. They wouldn't want them to watch programmes about drop-outs, drug addicts, or criminals. Eventually, that sort of information, fed into young people's minds, could pollute their thinking, attitude and behaviour, even to the point that they gradually destroy themselves. What you see and what you do affects your thinking, which affects your future.

Successful and loving parents encourage their children in positive activities, and maintain this as part of their daily routine.

Recently, on a weekend trip to France I came face to face with the reality that we all have a freedom of choice and sometimes the consequences of not taking advantage of available opportunities. On the ferry I met one of the guys from Calne under 17's football team that we played for when we were teenagers. During our conversation we reminisced about how great it was to be part of the team. Even though we had left school and gone into different jobs and colleges we still kept together as a unit. We trained together twice a week and played two matches each week. We went to parties and night clubs together and brought our girl friends along. We were a popular team, winning most games. Our whole lives revolved around the team.

Then, in one game against Corsham, a minor fracas broke out on the pitch and it turned into a full-scale fight. Because we were so close, we all supported one another in the fight. It may not have been the right thing to do but the closeness of the team meant no one could simply turn their back on what was happening but just had to get involved and help. The team was banned from football for a year. This more or less led to the break-up of the team.

The guy told me that, from that football team, three were dead, some were in jail, three worked in a factory and he was a plasterer. Membership of that squad had a very powerful effect on us all but the unity was through football alone. It was that which held us together. I was the only one to break away from the group. I am most definitely NOT sorry that my life took a different direction. Looking back now it was the best thing that could have happened to me. However, I do value the lessons I learnt in that football squad. They have given me a good perspective of how life can be. I believe that now I relate to many more people.

One of my most celebrated opportunities and privileges was meeting Robert Kiyosaki, the author of "Rich Dad Poor Dad", "Cash Flow Quadrant" and other best selling books. We were both speakers at a conference in northeast England. During the course of our interactions I learned a great deal from him about getting the most from both good and bad that happens in life. I encourage everyone that I know to read about him and how he was able to utilize his personal strengths to create opportunities that did not exist before. At the time we met he was in the process of buying an oil rig. He did not want to manage it himself but simply to receive an income of a few cents for each barrel of oil it produced. This is residual income. He has developed some business board games. He also teaches at business conferences around the world. By now I expect he is more than likely a billionaire. Many people would say: "Well look at him now, he's wealthy, he's successful." But they don't realise that in the early days, after he completed his military service and finished college, he and his wife lived in a car for several months because they pursued a dream. He refused to get a job despite his parents' encouragement. He refused to be like everybody else. Their families were saying things like: "Get a job like the rest of us, you can join us."

Robert Kiyosaki and his wife pursued their dreams with a sense of purpose, day in day out, and they went on to become very wealthy.

Success is just tough enough to separate the people who really want it from those who think they do. At the conference I had an opportunity to lunch with Robert Kiyosaki. His briefcase was bulging at the sides. He had lots of books and tapes on different subjects; his intention was to move on, even from his current position. He wanted to continue improving what he did each day, his 'routine'.

If you really want to move on and you want a mentor, you need to find someone you can trust who is where you want to be but is happily discontented and still moving on. These are the people you need to associate with, to learn their habits for success.

My good friend Geoff Thompson once used to sweep a factory in Coventry. At that time he had a dream and a goal to write one book in his lifetime. He has since written 30 books, produced videos and also DVDs. One of his short films won a BAFTA award. It just gives you an idea how people from different backgrounds can do so much more when they set their minds to something. Look at him now and you can see he's successful. He makes programmes for TV, radio and writes for magazines.

He wrote his first book while still working in the factory. He had the idea of writing a book and could picture the front cover with his name and see it in a bookshop. He realised he needed someone to help him. So he found some local authors and they gave him tips on how to write a book. Everyday he wrote just a few pages, he reviewed it, had it edited and published. His first book was in the shops.

Geoff Thompson explained the simple five step process he took:

1   He had an idea to write a book.

2   He visualised his name on the front cover.

3   He needed a coach, so he contacted some authors.

4   He wrote at least one page each day, in his daily routine.

5   He reviewed his writing and asked someone to read it.

It's the same as anything else. But he did say that his work colleagues in the factory wanted him to get ahead, but not ahead of them. So it's a natural thing that people will try to hold you back.

I also learned that sometimes even recognizing an opportunity might not be enough. Sometimes we become complacent or too comfortable so it can feel "scary" to leave the comfort and move on toward something better. Some people may be happily discontented. They appear to be happy on the surface but deep down they know that they want more out of life. I know how they feel; I felt the same way too. I had a secure career with a good future. I had signed on as a regular in the Royal Air Force. I was living a dream of being paid to play sports here and overseas and also to teach sport. Then I saw an opportunity. It was one that I could start in my spare time. Once I had built the business I found that it provided more income (from my spare-time work) than my job. So I decided to leave the secure military environment to continue with and expand my business and start others. There were times when I questioned whether I was doing the right thing. Many people are happily discontented but do not have the opportunity to create another income. There are those who are just happily discontented and yet simply put up with it.

For me, I would rather go into something with everything I have and give it my best efforts than to be like those who, on their death bed think: "if only…."

When we find a new opportunity that we think we can do, we must do everything we can to put our best efforts into it to succeed. Sadly, many people look at opportunities and see them only as problems. They do not realise that one definition of a problem is: "A solution in disguise".

Whenever my sons come to me with a problem, the first thing I do is to ask them what they think is the solution and why they think that one is correct. This helps to train their thinking for solutions and not to dwell on problems.

I include here as an illustration a personal challenge I faced. Some people might say: "It's OK for you, but you don't understand my situation." My situation was that I lived in a nice house in the country, not far from the city. At the time it was my dream house, set in several acres with seven bedrooms, six bathrooms, indoor swimming pool, a games room, and a bar. A manageable back garden of approximately one acre included a tennis court and a skate board ramp for the children. The front drive was big enough to park 15-20 cars. To me this was ideal. I was very happy with the choice of house and, through my daily routines; I was able to develop my business.

My whole working life, everything I had worked for, was tied up in that house. Gradually, however, it became clear that our marriage was breaking up beyond repair. At the separation the court decided, in the interests of the children, that they would be better served by living more with me than their mother. Therefore I became their main carer. This was a new situation - leaving a lovely house to move into rented accommodation close to the boys' school.

Many people have to go through challenges in life. Each one is different, whether it's losing a loved one, a tragic accident, redundancy or even a difficult divorce. I can identify with your situation when it seems that the carpet is suddenly whipped from under your feet.

From that mess in my life, I used the opportunity to develop stronger and deeper bonds with my sons and my mentors and those that really cared and supported me. I began again, to rebuild my life; I was a positive parent to my sons and maintained their lifestyle i.e. private education and sports interests. As their father I am there to help them through life's challenges.

From this situation you can take one of two views: you can be a moaner or a mover; you choose. I chose to move on hence the reason for this book. I believe passionately in the principles and the examples I give in this book. They have been learnt over the years from successful people in different businesses and cultures. They have strengthened me to move on from any situation. In life I can feel sorry for myself and have a pity party or I can make the most of every opportunity.

Successful people accept responsibility.

I cannot blame anybody else; I cannot blame life for the cards I have been dealt. I can just make the best of every situation, good or bad, in which I find myself. My hope is that this is the message that you, dear reader, will take from this book.

Opportunity is everywhere and as a military friend once told me; Times, Tides, Formations and opportunity wait for no one. Many people see opportunities but fail to recognise them for what they are. They put off until tomorrow the things they think they don't have to do today. Think of the great athletes of today, or the ones we remember from the past. For instance, think of Mohammad Ali, at the peak of his boxing career, do you think he spent less time in the gym or more than average? To get where he did, he had to do a lot more.

Recently I heard an interesting statistic about boxing: of the total time spent in preparation for a fight 98% is in training and 2% is in the ring. You will probably find that this is true in most endeavours in which a person has to perform. So you need to be prepared to work more effectively and, therefore, faster and more productively.

Opportunities do come to those who look for them.

A couple of years ago I was very fortunate to have an opportunity to work with Earnie Shavers. I did his personality profile for him. After that I helped him prepare after-dinner speeches.

Earnie Shavers was a boxing legend, known as the heaviest puncher in heavyweight history, during the time when Muhammad Ali, Joe Frazier, George Foreman and Ken Norton were all big names in boxing. Earnie Shavers still holds the record in heavyweight boxing for the ratio of the number of knockouts per fight. Even though he was an extremely strong and gifted boxer he lacked confidence in certain areas. He has always been well respected by everyone, since he took up boxing at the late age of 22 years. From a humble beginning as a cotton picker in Ohio, he entered the boxing world and rose to his highest point of fighting Muhammad Ali in Madison Square Garden. He believes that if he had had more confidence and if more people had believed in him when he was young, he would have gone on to win the World Heavyweight Championship against Muhammad Ali in 1977. From his youth he has led a very clean life; he has never drunk alcohol or touched drugs. Now, as an ordained minister, he still has his personal motto as: "Keep your name clean".

Earnie Shavers has collected a wide range of memorabilia from the great events during his boxing days. He has taken advantage of the opportunity to be a great friend of Muhammad Ali.

Key lesson

Consider your opportunities.

1   Am I looking daily for opportunities to change my life?

2   Would I be ready if an opportunity showed up today?

3   Do I want to do more than I am doing right now?

4   Do I have an ambition to do or be something special?

5   Can I see clearly what it is that I want?

6   Who do I ask to tell me more about my ambition?

7   Is there someone I know who could be my mentor?

8   Does my TV/DVD viewing help me towards my goal?

9   Am I reading books, listening to CDs to help me towards my goal?

10   Do I really want to succeed?

11   Does my routine include a review of each day's activities?

 **WHAT I HAVE LEARNT TODAY**

USE GOALS

Day 3

Use Goals - to a Destination

"Personal goal setting is the strongest force in the world."
Paul J Meyer

"What you get by reaching your goals is not nearly as important as what you become by reaching them."
Zig Ziglar

Today the subject is **USE GOALS**. Having seen an opportunity we now need to use goals to move us in that direction. We use the goal to motivate us into action. You will find that the bigger your dream the more energy, effort and enthusiasm you will put into achieving it. The more you want it, the more determined you will be.

Imagine for a moment that you know where you want to be, what you want to be doing. Imagine also that you expect to achieve it. You desire to be the best you can be in your chosen business or profession. When you feel that way, you will do all you can to learn as much as possible about the subject. In your daily routine you will feed your mind with the information that will help you. Successful people focus on what they want to achieve, and have an unwavering faith and belief that they will make it. It's how they think that gets them there. Of course, they weren't born thinking they were winners. They practise thinking that way, seeing themselves winning. They make a habit of visualising themselves as successful. They include in their daily routine a time to focus on their goal. It's just practice. They achieve success by habitually changing what they think. Also they change their effort to reach their goals.

This is their antidote to:

Same old, same old – by Tony Evans

Every day you get out of the same old bed and go to the same old bathroom to look at the same old face in the same old mirror.

You go to the same old closet to choose the same old clothes, and then sit down at the same old breakfast table to eat the same old breakfast.

Then you go to that same old garage and get into the same old car to head down that same old road to that same old job.

There you work all day for that same old pay, next to those same old people, supervised by that same old manager. Then you get into that same old car and head back down that same old road to that same old house.

Once you are home you sit down in that same old chair to watch that same old television. At the end of the day you go to that same old bed and sleep that same old way, so you can get up the next morning and start the same old routine all over again.

The daily routine above describes a life without purpose.

A good place to start making changes in your daily routine is in setting personal goals for different areas of your life. At the end of this chapter there are two tables for you to consider. Table 1 gives typical examples of areas in lifestyle that could be changed. Naturally, you need to have a desire to make changes before you attempt to make your own list of personal goals in Table 2. Let's say you want to change from your present income to another level in a certain time. To achieve this you will need to

40

plan the route, the actions you will take, to lead you to your target income.

Consider your work situation. If you feel that your work does not give you the satisfaction you would like, let's say less than five on a scale of one to ten, perhaps you need to do something about it. This is where knowledge of your personality style, your skills and interests will be very helpful.

In the summer of 2004, I was approached by Ron Headley, a former West Indies cricketer. His father was a legend, the great George Headley. His son, Dean Headley, also played test cricket for England. Ron wanted me to spend time with some of the West Indies team at Edgbaston in Birmingham. The goal was to work with the non-batsmen in the cricket team. For anyone who does not follow cricket (most people) there are 11 players in a team, the top 6 or 7 are batsmen and the rest the wicketkeeper and bowlers. When 10 players are out the team is out.

At the time the West Indies captain was Brian Lara, one of the greatest cricketers of all time. During the one-day internationals for the West Indies he was running out of batting partners. I was asked to help batsmen 7-11 to stay in and support Brian Lara so he could score more runs. My goal was not to help these guys with their technique. (How could I? I had never played test cricket.) but, more importantly, their tactics in working with Brian Lara. I worked on their performance gap. This is the difference between where they could be and where they currently were. I did this by averaging the scores in the previous ten games. I also asked the coach where he thought they could be, and then asked the players to write down where they thought they could be.

From this, for each player, we had a starting point; the average of ten games, the goal of the coach and the individual player's goal. So, for example, if somebody had a potential 6 out of 10 and was performing at 2 or 3 the goal was to give them guidance to think and believe they could be a 4 or 5. With all the batsmen from 7-11 increasing their scores by, maybe, 10-15% it would add another 30-40 runs to the team's score. More importantly they would spend time at the crease with the legend, Brian Charles Lara. This game plan worked because a month later in 2004, they went on to win the ICC world championship trophy at the Oval, beating England. It was the non-batsmen who were there to finish the job off!

I had changed their thinking and their daily routine to help them believe and work on a game plan that they could develop in more detail. This goes to prove again the principles of "Your success is hidden in your daily routine" can apply in any area of your life.

By changing your thinking and your daily routine, you can realise the goals you set yourself.

Your daily routine can include learning from the right people, personal experience, books and papers, tapes, DVDs, and CDs.

It is all very well to learn everything about your chosen field and to memorise every aspect in detail but there comes a time when you have to put that knowledge into action. This is the time when your daily routine changes and your whole life changes for the better.

Whatever you do in your work you will find that competence comes with practice.

Different people find certain subjects easier to learn than others. For instance, during my school days, I found sports easier and more enjoyable than mathematics or science. This is because I practised sport in preference to spending time studying mathematics. I'm sure that a good footballer would not consider himself to be a natural accountant. However, with an expert instructor and time to practise, the footballer could become competent at accountancy. Naturally, he must first have a burning desire to learn to be good with numbers. Otherwise it will be like trying to teach a pig to sing. You get frustrated and the pig gets annoyed.

One frequently quoted definition of success is the progressive realisation of a worthwhile goal. Simply expressed, a goal is a dream with a date attached to it, backed up with actions geared to make it happen.

Success does not suddenly turn up overnight. It is the result of a daily routine that is inextricably linked to a purpose. Looking back over my own life I can see that having personal goals made me put in the requisite effort, monitor my progress and achieve them. This has also been true of all (yes all) the successful people I have had the good fortune to meet.

After I left school I played in the Wiltshire under 19s cricket team. This was until I joined the Royal Air Force. Then I set myself a new goal to be in the Royal Air Force cricket team and it wasn't long before I met that goal.

Later, after leaving the Service, my business interests took a higher priority than cricket. Because of my work cricket had almost slipped out of my mind. Then one day, I met Alan Crouch, the coach for the Wiltshire under 15's cricket team. During our conversation he suggested that I apply to join the Marylebone Cricket Club (MCC), a prestigious club with its headquarters at Lord's cricket ground. Having not played for some time it seemed to me a very useful target.

Alan, ("Crouchie" as he is known) had helped me tremendously in cricket when I was fifteen. Later I went back to him to continue developing my cricket skills. (At times we have choices to make when different people can help us. At other times we stay with what has worked in the past. It can save time.) Alan's no-nonsense, direct coaching, style suited my personality. He kept things very simple and to the point. In any profession, especially in advanced technologies, there is a danger that the coach can give information overload in an effort to impress the student with the extent of their knowledge. This does not help the student.

I practised and stretched myself for two years, a sort of probation period. My new goal was to become a member at Lord's, a prestigious cricket club.

If I had not set this particular goal for myself I would not be playing cricket and coaching now. The knock-on effect is that I have met many great people. My sons also have the benefit of going to Lord's with me. It has inspired them in their cricket at school. They have both been accepted into a county cricket youth team. Who knows? They may wish to belong to the MCC as well when they are older.

Focus

Another difference that marks successful people is their ability to focus on what they are doing, where they are going, what they want, or what they want to be. It is as if everything they do has a goal or a target.

Let's take a simple example such as losing weight. Imagine that you want to shed, say, 20lbs or 9 kilos of weight. Some people might regard this as impossible. How can you lose 20lbs in weight? That's nearly one and a half stones in Imperial weight. They could never imagine that they could do it. If you think you cannot do it overnight, you're probably right. If you think you cannot do it at all, you're probably right as well. But, if you break it down, you can set yourself a start date and a finish date. If you're a guy you can visualise yourself, maybe in your swimming trunks; or if you're a lady, in your bikini on holiday. If you use a realistic goal, something you know you could achieve; maybe to lose 20 lbs in 20 weeks, suddenly it doesn't seem to be so difficult; it's just 1lb a week which is only a few ounces each day.

Life is much simpler and goals are easier to achieve if you break down the activities into your daily routine.

By focusing on the goal, regularly visualising yourself achieving it, your doubts will disappear and you will do what it takes to achieve it. You will have the discipline to work consistently and until you get there.

Allan and Barbara Pease are best-selling authors and have been on TV many times talking about relationships. Some time ago, Allan was diagnosed with cancer. For many people this would have seemed to be very tragic indeed, but what he did was to focus on something positive. He visualised enjoying several birthdays reaching into his 90s. He pictured what he would be wearing and who he would be with, whereabouts in the world he would be. He was so confident and optimistic about overcoming this challenge that he had his thigh tattooed with the statement: "good until ......" followed by a date.

The reason he did this was that it helped him to programme his mind for success to achieve a longer life. He knew that he would see the tattoo every time he had a shower. Obviously he also took medical advice, changed his diet, changed to organic food and it was no surprise to him that he recovered within a couple of years. He had some tests that declared him to be completely clear of the cancer. He has even set himself a goal to write a book about how he overcame cancer.

You can achieve anything by focusing on success, regularly. That will then change your action.

Earnings

It is often said that money comes third to oxygen and water. Whether we like it or not we need money. Some people say that they don't. They are only looking at their own minimal needs instead of the needs of other people, how they could help if they had more.

In her lifetime, Mary Seacole experienced riches and poverty. She expressed her view on money in her *"Wonderful Adventures"*:

45

"I never thought exclusively of money, believing rather that we were born to be happy, and that the surest way to be wretched is to prize it over much."

Here's something, which might surprise you. At first I found it quite disturbing because it was so very, very accurate in my own situation. Think about the five people you spend the most time with. They may be work colleagues, possibly in your social life, even in your family; the people you are happy to be with most of your time. They could be from next door or the local club or pub, maybe someone from your church. Write down those five names and your best guess of what you think their incomes might be. Add the figures together and divide the total by five. The answer should be quite close to what you are earning right now. Do this with ten of your closest friends and associates and you could find the answer to be more accurate.

Why? It's how we spend our time that matters. The people we associate with have a big influence on what we do and how we think. For example, attending business conferences can expand your mind if you want to have a big business. You meet with and listen to people who are successful from different backgrounds and different lifestyles. They can help you stretch your mind to enable you to grow to a new level.

Training conferences and information from mentors give you the roots to grow and the wings to fly.

If anyone wants to be successful in any venture, at some stage they need to learn and change a few things in their daily routine, so they can get on track to live the life they desire. It is the desire to change that becomes your motivation to do something different.

As a fitness coach I have met many people who say they want to make changes in their physical appearance. Some people talk about it; others make the changes. On one occasion a lady in the gym explained to me how she would like to be in better shape but had insufficient time to train, she was serious about this. She was a single parent with two children at school. After returning from work and preparing their food she had no time for the gym. Previously, other instructors had advised her to set up a gym at home. They had understood only part of her problem.

I spent an hour asking questions and listening. The children needed healthy food and she wanted to train. My recommendation was for her to have a chef-friend do bulk cooking for her to freeze. She could then thaw it during the day and microwave it at tea-time. This gave her an additional 7 hours in a week; enough for her to train 3 times a week. Her family didn't suffer and she enjoyed good health.

Remember, it's not big changes that count nor expensive equipment, it's making the right changes that make a difference.

Sources of Income

In his book *"Cash Flow Quadrant"* Robert Kiyosaki describes some extensive research that he carried out to see how people earn money. He found that 95% of the working population is made up of employed and self-employed people. They earn their money by selling their time and skills to create income. The higher the skills a person has in his or her work the more money he or she can earn. There is also a scarcity value for those specialists who are few and far between. Naturally, there is a limit on the available time that they can sell and, therefore, an upper limit on their income.

The other 5% are independent business owners and investors. These people invest money to create time. They do not work for money; their money works for them. The irony of this eye-opening situation is that the 95% share only 5% of the total available income whereas the remainder is available to the smaller group. I was quite alarmed when I first discovered this.

You may be surprised to see the following figures, collected over the last three decades. They were reported in one of the Sunday newspapers not so long ago. It was a survey on workforce earnings in the United Kingdom and Ireland.

(a)   The people earning below £10,000 made up 56.6% of the working population.

(b)   22.8% earned between £10,000 and £19,999. If the average income then was around £22,000 you can see that almost 80% of the working population earned below this figure.

(c)   10.9% earned between £20,000 and £29,999 a year.

(d)   6.2% earned between £30,000 and £49,999 a year.

(e)   1.9% earned between £50,000 and £99,999 a year.

(f)   That left just 1.6 % of people who earned in excess of £100,000 a year.

If you have an ambition to be in any one of these earning brackets, you need to develop a very good reason for wanting that level of income. If you have a job it's not necessarily that secure is it? So you may be interested in increasing your net worth by developing another income stream. There is no point in doing this if it's just the money that motivates you.

Remember, money is just a tool; it is neither good nor bad. It is the love of money that can cause all sorts of problems between people and in families.

When you make it a daily routine to focus on your desire, see yourself there, your mind will enable you to apply the necessary effort to get you there. Determination develops through practice. You may be surprised when you realise how much money is available and how few people make it. Do you think that anyone in the top 1.6% is more intelligent than everyone else? Probably they are not. Do you think they are more qualified than everyone else? Not necessarily.

I suggest that there are five things that they do consistently, as part of their daily routine that others don't.

1   They have a clear idea of what they want. They have a vision, a dream, an ambition, call it what you will, that will take them on the journey beyond their present position; it is their reason why they think they should progress.

2   They visualise it in their mind. They verbalise it out loud to themselves. Deep down, they believe that they can and will achieve it.

3.   They have a plan to take them to that dream and a burning desire to learn more about their chosen field. To do this they have a mentor, or coach, somebody who has already achieved what they want, or they are in touch with somebody who has achieved it. They also have a mindset that they will do whatever it takes to achieve their goal. They do not have a "9.00 to 5.00" mentality.

4   They have a consistent daily routine and a system which they are prepared to follow. They do this day in, day out, not just on those occasions when they feel good.

5   Each day they review their routine, progress, and goals.

Let's recap on that:

The top 1.6 per cent of earners know what they want; they can visualise it and believe they will achieve it; they have a mentor; they have a daily routine, a system which they review daily so they know where they are going.

You can use this in any or every area of your life.

A change in your thinking and your daily routine can change the position or the income bracket that you are in, or even your ability in work, hobbies and leisure activities.

Table 1 below shows an example of progress from starting points to final destinations for different areas of a person's life. This is an opportunity for you to think of your present situation; your starting points in your own life. You can set your own target destinations and the dates by which you aim to achieve them.

Table 1   Example of Personal Goals to a Destination

Life Style	Starting Point	Final Destination
Earned Income	£20,000	£100,000
Health	Average	Above average
Weight	13st (82.5kg)	10st (63.5kg)
Relationship- partner	OK	Excellent
Relationships - work	OK	Excellent
Time alone	2 hours per week	5 hours per week
Work (on a scale 1- 10)	4	9
Credit Card	On limit	Cleared monthly
Debit card	Overdrawn	Balance all month
Leisure time (hobby)	2 hours per week	8 hours per week
Holidays	Budget package	Own choice

Table 2 below is for you to write down your present starting points; your target final destinations and your target dates when you plan to achieve them. These goals are your own; your motivation to make changes in your daily routine. You can add other areas of your life for which you want to set personal targets.

Table 2   **My Personal Goals to a Destination**

Life Style	Starting Point	Final Destination	Target Date
Earned Income			
Health			
Weight			
Relationship- partner			
Relationships - work			
Time alone			
Work (on a scale 1- 10)			
Credit Card			
Debit card			
Leisure time (hobby)			
Holidays			

Key lesson

Consider the goals you use.

1   Do I know where I'm heading?

2   Do I use goals to move me into action?

3   Have I broken down my goals into manageable pieces?

4   Have I learnt all I can about my chosen work?

5   Do I focus on what I am doing?

6   Am I happy to tell others about my work or profession?

7   What income level do I want to achieve and why?

 # WHAT I HAVE LEARNT TODAY

TIME WITH MENTOR

Day 4

Time with Coaches and Mentors

"They call it coaching but it is teaching. You do not tell them it is so. You show them it is so."   Vincent T. Lombardi

"It is not so much our friends' help that helps us, as the confident knowledge that they will help us."   Epicurus

Today we consider **TIME**, particularly time with mentors. Having determined our goals we need to spend time with a coach or mentor.

'When the student is ready the teacher will appear.' A good mentor is invaluable as you set and develop your personal goals. He or she can lead you round the pitfalls and obstacles that would otherwise keep you from your dream if you were left alone.

When we are young we believe that anything is possible.

During early childhood we believe we can be anybody we like from an Olympic champion to an astronaut, a film star or pop idol. My first ambition was to be a premier league professional footballer. I knew I could succeed right to the premier league. Then, at age ten, I shelved the idea. I concluded that I would have to be exceptionally good, much better than I was at the time, to make the grade in the premier league.

What I didn't understand at the time was that the top players had a burning ambition to succeed in their game. They practised all the hours they could find. More than likely they had an excellent mentor or coach. They had someone who believed in them, encouraged and helped them to overcome their obstacles. A mentor is someone who has already succeeded in your chosen field and knows the journey upon which you have embarked. While your ambitions are young in your mind they are like young plants that need to be fed and nurtured. A good mentor will see potential in you that could be beyond your vision.

You need to feed your ambitions with passion, excitement, enthusiasm and knowledge.

When we have an idea of what we most desire or want to become, we set about finding out as much about it as we can. It is utterly pointless to ask somebody's advice if he knows nothing about the subject. All too often we come across people who ask for advice from their friends or acquaintances in the pub. I know because that is just how I did it. What we must do is to ask people who have experience in that particular field or career. We must then go and see, touch and witness whatever is our desire. If we are still convinced it is what we really want then we have to invest time, effort and, possibly money into whatever it is.

This is the time when you start to learn more about people who have succeeded in your chosen field. I remember my school days when I wanted to learn more about top people in sport. At that time my only sources of information were sports pages in newspapers.

At different times in my life I have had different mentors. I have found that in each area of my life, there are people, skilled in a particular aspect, who have taught me, helped me and guided me round the pitfalls. Their skill may be quite different whether it is physical fitness, finance, computing, relationships, spiritual, or work.

In the Royal Air Force my mentor was my coach, Bobby Quantock. To me he was the best instructor at my PTI course at Cosford. When I first joined the Service I was disorganised. I had no dress sense, no routine. The basic training certainly tidied me up and gave me some degree of organisation to the day.

Bobby Quantock, introduced self-discipline and routine in my sports training and other aspects of life.

To me he was a model PTI, immaculately dressed and with a great attitude. He was not particularly popular but I related to him because he was a straight talker and he got results. He helped me to develop discipline and routine. Looking back I realise that, without my time in the Royal Air Force, I could have easily slipped back into the sloppy habits learnt from the previous friends I hung around with.

When I think of three basic qualities required for a mentor to be really effective, honesty is first on the list.

A mentor needs to be honest and demonstrate integrity; someone you can trust; someone who will always do and say what is right in any situation.

The next important quality is competence in their subject. Bobby certainly knew how to get results in training PTIs.

Competence is not just knowing the subject, it is also the ability to read a situation, act appropriately and make decisions with wisdom.

The third quality is the person's personality; a mentor needs to be able to relate well and communicate with other people in the organisation.

It is especially important for both the student and mentor to understand one another and communicate well, being thoughtful and kind, rather than selfish and self-centred.

From personal experience it is important for everyone to have different mentors for different areas of their life. When you are a child you learn from your parents. However, as you grow up, you begin to understand that they cannot know everything about everything. I would not expect my fitness coach to advise me in business.

Earlier I mentioned the help that I have received from Dr Peter and Eva Muller-Meerkatz. To me they provide mentorship *par excellence*. They are a great encouragement in my life and businesses; wherever they are in the world they are always available to advise me. My vision for my future has broadened considerably as a result of what I have learnt from Peter and Eva.

A good friend of mine, Richard Taylor, is Assistant Pastor of my local church. I have heard him preach quite often and he is an excellent speaker. Once I asked him, at short notice, to speak at a conference. The subject was not in his area of expertise but I knew he was a brilliant speaker and communicator. We produced a motivational tape from the event. Since then he has spoken for us on other occasions and he now speaks to large audiences around the world. Without doubt he is a great speaker and an inspiration to many people. He speaks with conviction, energy and wit and it is a pleasure to be with him.

I am grateful to David Carr, the Senior Pastor who gives great wisdom and encouragement. David and Richard are a unique combination leading a very successful church with approximately 1500 people attending each Sunday. It is great for me to be able to tap into David and Richard as my spiritual mentors and for life wisdom. My children are also great friends with both of them.

It is wise to remember the following points when you look for the correct mentor to help you in your chosen field or any aspect of your life.

1.   *Is he or she where you want to be in this area?*

2.   *Is he or she quietly discontented and working to achieve higher levels?*

3.   *Does he or she have a coach who is at a higher level?*

"Ability is what you are capable of doing.

Motivation determines what you do.

Attitude determines how well you do it."

Lou Holtz

A supreme example of a top sportsman and coach was in the combination of Muhammad Ali and Angelo Dundee. Sometimes we look at extremely successful people and see their confidence. During his boxing career Muhammad Ali was an example of the best in his sport. We only have to mention his name anywhere in the world and a smile would appear on someone's face because he is universally recognised as one of the greatest sportsmen of all time.

Now who could be a mentor to such a man and give him confidence; who could encourage him and keep him training? His trainer was Angelo Dundee, a quietly spoken small guy of few words. He was always in the background when Ali was around.

Through his religious beliefs Ali decided not to go to war in Vietnam and accept the consequences. We must respect his views because he was prepared to give up everything. For his own personal views he served three years in jail, he gave up the World Heavyweight Championship title, arguably at the peak of his career. Later he returned to fight Joe Frazier for the World Championship.

Ali was under-prepared for the fight which went to fifteen rounds. In round fifteen Frazier knocked him down a couple of times and went on to win on points. Ali, beaten for the first time in his career, obviously shaken, had to go through preliminary fights again before he had the right to fight Frazier for the undisputed World Heavyweight Championship.

Their third fight was in July 1975. He called this the "Thriller in Manila". The temperature in the boxing ring was over 100^0F and the fight went to the fourteenth round in which Ali gave Frazier a tremendous punishing. He gave Frazier everything he had in him and thought that he would knock out Frazier but he was still standing at the end of the round.

Ali went back to his corner and said to Angelo Dundee: "There's absolutely nothing left in me. I know that if I go out there and he hits me once I will be on the floor. Don't let me do this." Angelo Dundee looked him straight in the eyes and slapped him hard across the face. He said to Ali: "You're a wimp. Now stand up." Remember it was over 100^0F in the ring. He made Ali stand up to his full height ready for the fifteenth round. Ali stood up. Frazier saw him standing there and immediately threw in the towel. Frazier could not go another round. The fact that Angelo Dundee motivated his protégé, when he was at his lowest, when he had absolutely nothing left in him, just to stand up is a great example of how the right mentor can appear at the right time.

In your own work or profession you will reach a point where you can teach others and share your skills and knowledge. If you have a good mentor you will duplicate the best aspects of his profession. Remember, and be aware, that any bad habits you have can easily be duplicated.

In any work or profession first learn, then do and then teach.

I have a saying for myself: "When you're up or motivated you need to go down and when you are low, or disheartened, go up." In other words, if you are a leader, coach or adviser, when you are at the top of your game you need to be around people you can help. Conversely, when you are at your lowest you need to go up to your mentor for inspiration and help.

If you want to learn new skills and expand your mind the tools may not necessarily be found in your own back yard. You may need to travel to learn from more successful people. You will need to be around people who have bigger mind sets to achieve greater success. Why? Because success does rub off and it is important that we have a bigger picture rather than a small one. If you want to be successful as a coach or mentor, in order to encourage your team, it is important that you are also inspired by other mentors and coaches. This keeps your mind fresh and open to other views.

Through my connections in cricket and from playing for the MCC I made friends with a cricketing legend, Mushtaq Mohammed. I say he's a legend because he played test cricket for Pakistan at age fifteen and a half, becoming the youngest test cricketer of his time. His test career spanned two decades and he captained his country. (Recently he wrote his autobiography, "Inside Out").

He was coach for Pakistan from 1995-1999. I had an opportunity to help him get Pakistan to the 1999 World Cup final. (Pakistan has high expectations of their cricket team.) Mushtaq approached me because of my knowledge in personality profiling. Through our discussions before the series I was able to advise him on organisation and working with the interpersonal skills of the squad. He needed some confidential support in respect of several high profile players. He needed them to work together, as a cohesive unit. Mushtaq is a mild-mannered gentleman and sometimes lacked the necessary forceful authority even though, quite clearly, he had walked the walk with his previous cricket experience. Now I couldn't have helped him in teaching cricket; I had never played it at test level. These players were super-stars. But I was able to show him how the team could work together, with harmony in the squad. He could then keep their egos in check to enable the team to achieve greater success.

During our conversations and by watching the coaching and net sessions, we developed a game plan. Pakistan went on to play in the final against Australia which was more than even Mushtaq Mohammed had expected. They reached their greatest achievement in World Cup cricket since 1991 when they won.

As a mentor I've learned that truth and integrity are far more valuable than short term gains.

That same year my family and I were living in a house set in seven acres of land. We planned to move and put the house up for sale. Several estate agents wanted to advertise it through magazines such as Country Life. One agent, David Milligan, was very sincere and I trusted him. His company's commission was the highest but I felt it was right to sign an exclusive deal with him. David was a charming man, and arranged thirty viewings. Unfortunately, no acceptable offer resulted.

Then by coincidence, I met a couple in a local pub; during the conversation they said that they were looking for a house like mine. They were not aware that it was on the market. They asked me to show them round but I encouraged them to arrange a visit through the estate agent. The lady who showed them round had a dominant personality. Unfortunately, the couple did not like her and wanted no further contact with the agent. They were prepared to offer more to deal directly with me. I contacted David Milligan and explained the situation. The sale was in danger of collapse simply through a personality clash! David completed the sale by dealing with the clients himself.

We do business with people we like, so successful people develop likeable qualities.

I could have saved a lot of money in that deal but it would have been only for that single transaction. David has since advised me on other property deals for no charge, respecting my trust in him. The amount of money he has saved me since that sale has far outweighed the short term benefit I might have gained. And I can sleep better knowing that I did the right thing without short-changing anyone.

Successful people work with coaches, even when they are high achievers. They continue to strive to be more, and value coaching to reach bigger goals.

During my career in the Royal Air Force one of my detachments was at Hereford. I was asked to mentor some older students. These guys were in their middle 20's. Normally I had worked with younger trainees between 16 and 20. I've worked with many elite groups, but there seemed something different about this one. I thought they were slightly arrogant but they were also incredibly fit. My goal is to stretch people so they improve in every area of life. I used to do this by waiting until one or two broke down or became exhausted or even sick. This wasn't something I'm proud of but it is just what we inherited by pushing people to their limits. One thing I noticed about these guys was that they didn't seem to *have* any limits. The harder I pushed them the more they carried on. Their attitude could be called 'bullet-proof' - they could not be broken.

Later I found out they were part of the elite Special Air Service. They never mentioned it at the time; it was through circumstances I found out. I questioned one of the guys that there was something different about him. He explained that they were the Special Air Service. The way he said "special" had a magic ring to it.

Successful people rarely say who they are - their actions speak for themselves.

Years later I was fortunate enough to host and speak at a conference with a former SAS legend, Sir Ranulph Fiennes. One thing he said to me was that he had always been an individual; he had always bucked the system. "But," he said "When it comes to life and death situations every trained SAS member, or even any individual, will have a routine and system that he will use on auto-pilot in times of desperation." He said there were times during his extensive travels when he was on minimal energy in adverse conditions. His higher functions switched off, but for survival he went on to 'auto-pilot' and relied on a learned system and routine, which made the difference between life and death. So, elite people like the SAS use a system. It happens to be far beyond anyone else's. But if it works for people who we rely on in life and death situations don't you think a routine could help us in being more productive in our jobs, studies, career, or relationships?

These are the people who take living to the next level.

Another responsibility as a mentor is to continue your own personal growth in order to help others get to where they want or need to go. I recently attended a team-building event at Manchester United:: "United in Business". John Shiels was speaking in relation to Manchester United's core values. When Manchester United selects players they look for 4 basic disciplines that any professional footballer needs: Physical, Mental, Tactical and Technical. But they pay a premium for the 3 Ts - Twist, Turns and Tricks. These abilities cannot be taught, they are natural gifts.

I run corporate team-building events for some clients; in football, in cricket at Lord's and rugby at Twickenham. As a result I have been fortunate to learn some of the core values of successful teams. As mentors and coaches, it is important for us to give people the basic skills in their chosen fields and then allow them to use their own natural abilities.

It is unsurprising that this philosophy at Manchester United has not changed over the years, when you consider some of the great stars who have worn the United shirt: George Best, Dennis Law, Bobby Charlton, Eric Cantona, Ryan Giggs, Cristiano Ronaldo and David Beckham to name but a few.

So my message to mentors and coaches is to let people express themselves within the routine of your own structure.

Rewards

It is important to reward yourself for goals achieved not only for yourself, but also for those around you. Be sure that the reward is appropriate to the goal and that you really deserve it. If you don't reward yourself, the people who work with you could despise your work - they may think you are making the work appear more important than its rewards.

A good mentor will remind others that it is important to reward oneself for goals achieved by oneself as well as the group. However, when I achieved a particular goal, there were so many other things going on that it seemed crazy to reward myself with a holiday. I spoke with my business mentors and they advised me to take the holiday to fulfil the promise I had made to my family. I had achieved the goal and met the criteria set. If I had not taken the holiday the goal would not have been worth the effort. And my family would have felt let down. (Coaches and mentors can also stretch your mind about rewards). So we went to Bermuda for two weeks. To me Bermuda is out of this world, with its all round natural beauty. Just imagine luxuriant tropical gardens, shimmering pink sandy beaches, azure blue sea as far as the eye can see; with spectacular sunrises and sunsets. That's Bermuda!

We stayed at the Sonesta Beach Resort Hotel overlooking acres of land, sandy beaches and beautiful gardens. Imagine golfing with your children on picturesque Par 3 courses with waterfalls, landscaped gardens, greens and fairways; the sea and palm trees in the background. Imagine drinks wagons around the course for refreshments. This is how golf should be; unlike courses at home in the rain, mud, miserable and cold. This is the place to learn to play golf. The private beach alongside the hotel is just wonderful, it is raked every day. The water is a very clear turquoise and gives you an opportunity to enjoy the sea life.

An incident during that holiday made me realise that we must not take things for granted. Like any proud father I filmed my boys at different times. On one occasion Josh and I were on the beach, Luke was swimming. I was filming and zoomed in on Luke a fair distance out at sea. At first I thought he was in no harm, a good swimmer; he had passed his one mile test. But, as I watched him through the lens, I suddenly realized he wasn't making any headway towards the beach. He was in fact swimming against a strong current. Fully clothed, I immediately went into the water and swam out to rescue him. I reached him and could clearly see that he was struggling. All's well that ends well!

I mention this because there are times when we presume that people can perform certain tasks easily. However, that may not be the case. Whether you are an employer, parent or coach the situation is different. In this instance my complacency was the presumption that Luke would have no problem swimming in the sea. A mile in a swimming pool is clearly vastly different to a mile off the Atlantic coast.

Spending time with successful people had broadened my horizons, even about holidays. We went on a diving trip during that holiday. We had a glass bowl, like a diver's helmet, to wear over our heads. We went underwater and had air pumped around us. We went down in our swimming trunks. The instructor gave us little pieces of food and some awesome tropical fish came to us. We were able to touch the fish. It was an unforgettable experience. I am very grateful to have had such a holiday. The boys thoroughly enjoyed it as well. I could not have imagined being in Bermuda, visualising such rewards, without associating with mentors who had already been there.

Key lesson

Consider your time and your mentor.

1   *Am I ready for a mentor in my work or profession?*

2   *In which other areas in my life do I need help?*

3   *Have I found a mentor I can trust?*

4   *Does that person demonstrate honesty and integrity?*

5   *Is that person competent to help me in my subject?*

6   *How do I relate to that person?*

7   *How does that person relate to others?*

 **WHAT I HAVE LEARNT TODAY**

INVESTIGATE

Day 5

Investigate and be Responsible

"The price of greatness is responsibility."   *Winston Churchill*

Today we consider **INVESTIGATE** - the things you need to know. We have used goals to move forward, visualised success, spent time with a mentor and changed our daily habits. Now we need to be responsible for the knowledge and experience we gain.

Investigate where you are and take responsibility for your thoughts and actions. By visualising your goals, and taking responsibility to practise in your chosen field, you will develop winning habits to succeed.

Successful people accept responsibility for their lives, their work, their actions and whatever happens as a consequence of their actions. Their philosophy is:

"If it is to be, it's up to me."

The human race has lived in a blame culture since the beginning of time. When we blame someone else we are, in effect, handing power over to them. It is a way to avoid the truth about our own shortcomings.

Few people accept their responsibility nowadays. Bosses blame workers for poor performance, whilst workers blame bosses for poor management. Parents blame teachers for their children's lack of achievement/low grades, and teachers blame parents for not supporting children at home. Blaming each other wastes time, achieves little and builds resentment. Can you remember the last time that you were blamed for something you didn't think was your fault? With every year that passes society seems to blame more and accepts less responsibility. It's good business for lawyers but, in the end, we need to take responsibility for our actions and avoid blaming others, we need to make the best of those situations.

When you look at your own situation in depth and take responsibility for it, you take charge of your life and then you can change its outcome. By avoiding thinking about it and blaming somebody else, you hand over the controls.

If you want the best for you and your family, I suggest you start right now, reflect and take responsibility for everything in your daily routine. Decide what it is you want to achieve.

Some people try to blame their parents and their upbringing for their lack of success, or having the wrong start in life. These are simply excuses. Many of us can do that. My name, De Souza, is Portuguese; my dad was born in Kenya but his family come from Goa, India, a Portuguese colony. My mum comes from Cape Town and I was born in England. I grew up on council estates. My former wife's heritage is in the Caribbean. I don't regard any of these as disadvantageous. Quite the opposite I can genuinely support whichever country is winning in cricket or football. Incidentally, my brother lives in Australia. He had the courage to give up everything he had worked for and start again. Now he is a successful property developer in Sydney.

You can either make excuses or money, you can't do both.

Successful people take responsibility for where they are, at any time. There will always be exceptions, but ultimately, we are responsible for the position that we are in, whether we like it or not. Sometimes it may be good and sometimes not so good. By taking responsibility for our part we have a chance to move on. That's the starting point. Ask yourself if you are happy with your starting point; where you are now. If it's not where you want to be, without blaming anybody else, think of what happened, or what you did, what choices you made, to get you to this point. Now think how you are going to do better to overcome the challenges. Ask yourself what changes you need to make. Remember, every choice you make has an outcome, an end result that is either good or bad depending on your choice.

Think of a car satellite navigation system. To calculate a route the first thing it checks is its present location, your starting point. It determines this from the satellite information it receives. You input the destination, your goal, and then it calculates the route to get there.

Most of us know where we want to go. But if you don't know your starting point there is little chance of moving on.

"Everything seems to go wrong for a gloomy person but for a cheerful person everything seems right."   **Proverbs 15:15**

We are responsible for how we act and how we react in every situation.

Some people are enthusiastic. They have a smile on their face and see the bright side of life. They have a spring in their step and are attractive to others. They have a good self image and good relationships with others. They expect the best of themselves and all they do each day. How can we make this attitude part of a daily routine?

Making a Positive Attitude a part of a daily routine requires three key areas of Personal Responsibility

1   Service

To be a leader we must first learn to serve others.

One definition of success is that if you help enough people to achieve what they want you will become successful.

Reaching your life goals is your objective but what you become as a person is far more important as you help others reach their goals.

2   Appreciation, gratitude

People touch our lives in so many different ways. Showing our appreciation by face to face thanks, letter, phone call or e-mail is an essential part of our daily routine. This not only helps us in our relationships, but also how we feel about ourselves. Our response to a good turn must be genuine, not flattery or condescension. You can make it a habit to acknowledge people. As a daily routine, compliment someone (genuinely!) for something you like about them; a different person each day. You may have observed that successful people do this effortlessly, because they have made it a habit.

3   Self-Image

When you are confident of where you are going you will see yourself as already being there. Once your dream or vision is clear in your mind and you are convinced that it is right, you will live your dream. You will act as though you have reached it; all your efforts will be directed to fulfil it. When you have absolutely no doubts at all of who you are, you will not be tossed around by the fashions of the day. You will have no fear of failure; no one will be able to deter you from your chosen path. You can achieve this, even if it seems unbelievable today. By using the daily routines in this book, your habits and your thinking can change.

73

Like the mind the body needs to be fed regularly with the right sorts of foods and nutrition supplements.

Our body's shape and weight are directly related to the food we eat and the exercise we take.

It's as simple as that. It is also well known that our brain and our thinking also benefit from the right food and proper physical exercise. Exercise is an important part of your daily routine. The sooner you do it after you wake up, the earlier your body and brain will function to meet the needs of the day.

Take the example that you want to lose weight. You have a clear idea of the shape and weight you want to be. Maybe you set yourself a goal to lose ten pounds. You visualise how you would like to look. You could even cut out a photograph of your face and put it on a picture of a well-formed model and stick the combination on your fridge and say: "That's where I can be." It sounds a bit crazy but it works. You need to regularly visualise yourself as being that shape and size. Make it a habit.

You may need a coach, somebody to encourage you or who has already succeeded in a weight-loss programme. A fitness instructor can help you with your diet, nutrition and exercise. Develop a daily routine, to include what and when you eat. After all; *"We are what we eat."* Review your progress daily; maybe check your weight at the same time every day.

This little project gives you an idea. You could set goals in other areas of your life, and as you put it into your daily routine it will work for you and you will achieve success.

Let's say you are a person who lives an instant lifestyle. You want quick results, a quick fix and instant weight-loss. You see people who look in great shape and you would want to be like them. Wanting to lose 20lbs overnight, you buy an exercise machine, or a quick fix diet. To achieve your goals more quickly, all you need is to work more on your routine. If it's to lose weight then yes, it means eating less fat and exercising more often.

There are two main things a body does with fat – it either stores it or burns it.

The body doesn't throw fat away, because it never knows when its next meal will come. It has something like 30 billion fat cells all ready and waiting to store fat. A lot of them are round your waist. If, when you exercise you burn less fat than you eat it's natural that you will put on weight. Take responsibility for what you eat in your diet. Some people I have trained make excuses that they were late for work and the canteen only sold junk food. Are you really blaming the canteen for how you look? A recent survey said that 'good-looking' people make more money. So that would mean the canteen is responsible for your income. Take time to reflect, and change your routine, say; make your lunch the night before. When it becomes a habit you won't have to think about it. It will just be part of your daily routine.

Burning fat or storing it is your choice!!

Just think, have you ever seen an obese top athlete or sportsman? Maybe it's because their daily routines include a healthy balance between exercise and food intake.

Have you ever watched a marathon on TV? Perhaps you have run one yourself. Some people start a marathon complacent of the outcome and fail to finish the distance. Other runners seem to reach a limit before the end. It's called 'hitting the wall' and in a 26 mile (42km) marathon, it could happen at any time. The athletes don't know if they can continue. It is when they hit that wall, they need to visualise their goal and know why they're running. Without this they could give up prematurely. You may have seen two runners in a race who look equally fit, and yet one beats the other at the last. It's determined by how they are thinking whether they can overcome their 'wall'. Many top athletes have talked about this in interviews. They even have sports coaches just for mental training. We can apply these techniques in our lives too.

I believe that the reason we do something is much more powerful than how to do it.

My dad died when he was only 51. I thought: "Surely, not my dad, he was fit." He did have asthma but that was about all. I was devastated. Like me he was a keen sportsman. When he was younger he and I played in the same hockey team together. I couldn't imagine him dying at such a young age. What I didn't realise at that time was the effect that his daily routine of smoking and drinking was having on his body. Maybe even his eating and exercise habits were not the healthiest.

My dad's death came as a great shock. It set me thinking deeply about my own life. Why am I here? What is the purpose of my life? I discussed this with my younger brother and he suggested that I speak to our uncle who was a pastor. I began to ask him these questions. He helped me immensely by pointing out the spiritual dimension in life as well as physical and intellectual. This led to further discussions and reading. I became convinced of the importance of keeping a balance between the different activities that nurture the body, the mind and the soul in my daily routine. I feel that this change of thinking has benefited me and, as a result, has enabled me to help others.

I don't know how my dad felt towards the end of his life; physically, mentally and spiritually. It is quite possible that he did experience pain in all three areas. If he did he didn't let it show and he may have thought that it was not bad enough for him to do anything about it. This reminds me of a story of a dog in pain.

The Dog in Pain

One summer holiday a boy visited his grandfather in the country. He loved going to the country and spending time with his grandfather. The grandfather was very wise and was able to answer his grandson's questions with stories. They were sitting on the veranda, the grandfather in his rocking chair and the boy beside him. The big dog lay on the wooden floor.

The grandfather and the boy were in deep conversation when, suddenly, the dog emitted a loud whining howl. Alarmed, the boy asked: "What's up with the dog?" After a pause, the grandfather nonchalantly replied: "Well, you see, he is lying on a nail." "Then why doesn't he move?" asked the boy again. The grandfather shrugged his shoulders; "Well, I suppose the nail doesn't hurt him enough."

Many people are in a similar situation, just like the dog; they are hurting in their jobs and careers, but they are just not hurting enough to have the urge to do anything about it. It is very easy to be complacent and think you could move on if you wanted to. But you know how it is; we take a job, thinking it is temporary. Then we realise the job has commitments attached to it; family, mortgage, rent or other financial commitments. It's easier to carry on doing the same thing, stuck in the same routine. One year merges into another and without reviewing our progress or where we're going, we find we are just drifting along to retirement; living a life without any real purpose.

When you find yourself in this situation it is easy to blame other people but it is your responsibility. Each of us is responsible for what we make of our lives. We cannot allow others to make decisions for us and expect the outcomes to be in our favour.

It is possible to change. You don't have to be stuck in a rut, a part of the rat race, going no place fast. Investigate a different routine, a routine which can be developed so you can change your future for the better.

Consider men aged 65 years. Over the last few decades surveys in the UK have shown that up to 54% of men retire broke. They have to rely on the state or others to support them. Currently, there doesn't appear to be a reliable pension scheme, especially for those still working and particularly for those under the age of 40 years.

A further 36% of men do not actually survive to the normal retirement age.

As many as 5% of men lack savings and pensions. As a result they have to continue in some kind of work after retirement just to earn some income. Generally, they find themselves not the best jobs in the world, more often than not it is the sort of work that they're forced into just to provide a minimal income to survive.

The next 4% are financially independent. This means all their financial commitments are covered comfortably by a residual income. This is income from different sources irrespective of whether they work or not. After they have met all their commitments they still have some disposable income left.

The remaining 1% is really very wealthy.

The level of income that individuals have in retirement is directly related to how they handle their finances during their working lives as part of their daily routine.

At the turn of the last century not all women worked. Since then it has become more of a necessity for both parties to work. Child minders and nannies have become so popular now in our changing times along with cleaners, people who do the ironing, those who help in the house, gardeners and so forth. It's because the people with money are trying to create more time for themselves and their families. In the same way, those without money are trying to find ways by which they can create more money for themselves, even a small amount extra.

The Snake and the Boy

A snake and a boy were at the top of a mountain. The boy saw the snake shivering. The snake asked the boy: "Do you think you could please carry me down to the bottom of the mountain because it's cold up here and I am freezing?"

The boy replied: "Well, I could do that for you but if I do, you may bite me and I will die."

The snake said: "No, I wouldn't do that. If I did that, we would both die". The boy was a bit apprehensive, but in the end he said "Okay then, I'll try." He picked up the snake, put it in his arms and held it close to his chest and started walking down the mountain. Every step the boy took the snake got warmer and warmer and just before he arrived at the bottom of the mountain, the snake turned around and bit him. The boy sat back, collapsed and said: "I'm going to die! What on earth made you do that? I've just carried you all the way from the top of the mountain, I've saved your life and that's what you do to me". The snake turned to him and said: "You knew what I was capable of doing before you picked me up".

Many of us are holding that 'snake' without realising it. If you have a job, your employer has the potential to 'bite' you at any time. Your employer owes you nothing. Jobs for life now are very, very rare. If you have debts i.e. in the form of a mortgage, car finance, credit cards or a loan of any kind, the lender can 'bite' you at any time and call in the loan. If the 'snake' that you are holding does 'bite' you, it is your own fault, you knew what it was capable of doing before you agreed to carry it.

The Royal Shakespeare Company is one of the most prestigious acting companies in the world. Recently my younger son, Josh, had an opportunity to audition for a part in Macbeth. Almost for fun Josh wanted to go and I arranged to take him. Normally, for cricket trials, I would say to him: "Trained or untrained?" and he would reply: "Trained." I would encourage him by saying "Fine, just show them what you can do." For the audition it was different. He had very little notice and was quite unprepared. I asked him the usual question and, this time, his reply was: "Totally untrained." We laughed and he said: "All I can do is give it my best shot." I replied with: "Fine, enjoy yourself." He went in and came out with a broad smile and the part of Banquo's son, Fleance.

In life we cannot always be prepared for a specific event but we can prepare ourselves in other aspects of lifestyle such as confidence, attitude, and self belief. More often than not these will help to overcome most situations. It is not just the performance on the day. Josh may not have been prepared for the particular script but he was certainly prepared for the stage.

Often, when I organise conferences I invite Luke and Josh on stage just to say a few words. This has given my boys the confidence to speak in front of an audience and to mix with people and behave respectfully. By taking responsibility for your routines, you can gain confidence to handle new challenges.

Key lesson

Investigate, ask questions, and seek out the truth. Take responsibility.

1   *Do I investigate and think about my situation?*

2   *Do I accept responsibility for my situation?*

3   *Do I appear cheerful to others?*

4   *Whom do I serve?*

5   *Am I happy serving others?*

6   *Do I appreciate what others do for me?*

7   *Am I confident without being arrogant?*

8   *Is my eating and exercise in balance?*

9   *Is my weight right for my height?*

 **WHAT I HAVE LEARNT TODAY**

NEVER GIVE UP

Day 6

Never Give Up - Reset Your Goals

"Your life can't go according to plan if you have no plan."

E.C.McKenzie

Today we consider **NEVER GIVE UP**- When you've reached one goal create another to keep moving on. So far we have developed a daily routine to use goals, visualise success and work with a mentor. You have changed your routine, investigated and taken stock of your situation and taken responsibility for your actions and their outcomes. Now we need to see beyond our new-found situation and aim for another one.

Winston Churchill is one of the most famous people in modern UK history. Once he gave a speech, which many have heard about. He made the speech to the boys at Harrow School on 29th October 1941. He started: "Never, never, in nothing great or small, large or petty, never give in except to convictions of honour and good sense. Never yield to force; never yield to the apparently overwhelming might of the enemy."

The letter N in this chapter means: 'Never quit your daily routine.' There was an audio tape produced in which someone gave a complete talk for an hour just about the words 'never quit'.

He talked about the war and how it impacted individuals and society. It was brilliant! I simply say: "never quit". We don't have the time or space for it in this book and I couldn't be as passionate about using the word 'never' for a whole chapter.

A friend of mine, Glenn Smith, used to be a scaffolder. He is now a top boxing coach. I asked him what made him want to change from being a scaffolder to becoming a boxing coach. He replied that he had a dream of being at Madison Square Garden in the corner with the world champion. One day when that dream was big enough he decided to walk out of the scaffolding job to set up his own gymnasium where he would teach boxing. Several of his associates in scaffolding jobs tried to discourage him: "Hey, stay where you are, it's a safe position and it pays a lot of money." He wanted to pursue something which, for him, was far greater than scaffolding. He now has several expert coaches and trainers working with him including: Tony Somers, Paul Hudson and Matty Evans

When I wanted a career in the Military I needed mentors who could help me achieve that goal. So I associated with people who were already teaching sport there. I had a system in place for me to do the right training to become a Physical Training Instructor.

Then, after five years, I was happily discontented. I had almost outgrown the position. Are you in a similar situation? You've climbed the ladder of success in your company, your job or your career, just to find out you're not going any further or it's leaning against the wrong wall. It is not taking you where you really want to be in your life. You may have changed your ambitions, and it's never too late to do that.

Great Britain and Ireland are two of the best countries in the world for people to become wealthy and live their dreams. My business has enabled me to travel the world. One trip was to Cape Town, South Africa. From the hotel the magnificent sight of Table Mountain is clearly visible in the distance. Up on the mountain slope there is a little restaurant. One day I had breakfast there while preparing for the conference. The view from the restaurant is a breathtaking panoramic scene for miles around Cape Town. Your dreams and goals can take you anywhere.

At the end of the conference, I met some of the delegates and was amazed to find that, due to lack of transport, they had walked for several hours to attend. Some of the delegates lived in tin huts in the surrounding townships. Their desire to have a business of their own and to succeed was incredible. It made me realise how fortunate I was to live in Britain because we certainly don't have anywhere near the sort of challenges which people face in South Africa.

On another occasion I spoke at a conference in India. Afterwards I had an opportunity to watch a cricket match in which a great friend, Vinod Kambli was playing. After the match he and Sachin Tendulkar invited me out for dinner and the subject of the rich and poor divide came into the conversation. Clearly we don't have anywhere near the same disparity between affluence and poverty in the UK. The UK and Ireland offer so much more in the way of opportunities for everyone. When wealthy sportsmen and businessmen endorse the fact that we live in such a country of great opportunities, it just gives me a tremendous feeling that this really is a wonderful country for life and work. Somehow, not everyone sees opportunities because they are so often disguised as challenges. Yet I have met many people who have become very successful through working hard toward their goal.

Michael Fraser is an excellent example of someone who changed his daily routine to dramatically change his life. A great friend, he is a real inspiration. Michael has spoken at my conferences with great humility and sincerity. He is totally relatable and approachable.

He co-presented the hugely successful BBC TV's *'To Catch a Thief'* and *'Beat the Burglar'*. He was the Principal Mentor of Channel 4's *'Going Straight'* and he is regularly requested to contribute his expert opinion on *BBC Breakfast* and *GMTV*. Michael is also the author of the best selling anti-burglary book *'How Safe is Your Home?'*.

As a young man Michael came within a whisker of receiving a custodial sentence for burglary and has not forgotten how he could so very well have gone on to become a hardened criminal had he not been given a chance to 'go straight'. His childhood was not a happy one. He was put into care and immediately separated from his siblings.

He was moved constantly from home to home and expelled from more than one school. Eventually, he left school with little or no qualifications. In his early adulthood he drifted into petty crime and seemed to be heading down a steep and slippery slope, mixing with completely the wrong company.

Looking back to his youth, Michael recalls the real turning point in his life. The owner of a small aluminium company was prepared to 'take a risk' and employ him as a junior. Due to his sheer fright at the looming prospect of a jail sentence, Michael threw himself into his work. It was this humble beginning, sweeping the factory floor, which enabled him to earn an honest living. He moved into the production department and started making door frames, working early and finishing late increasing his daily production. From that position he decided to become self-employed. He then began to employ workers and has continued to move on to become the successful businessman today.

Procrastination

Procrastination is a great labour saving device "I'll do it later, tomorrow, sometime, one day." is a common expression.

I am sure that there are some of you reading this book who have a task that should have been done by now. But you have thought to yourself: "I'll get around it to it one day." Maybe it's a letter you should respond to or something you have said you would do for somebody else. Letting it slip is easily done isn't it? Why is it that we put things off so much?

Imagine winning an exotic holiday on an island in the sun. The phone rings and a voice at the other end announces: "Well, the good news is you are the lucky winner of a holiday in the sun. It's for two weeks at our expense and you have to leave tomorrow." Your first concern may well be whether your boss will let you have the time off work. Imagine that your boss then phones saying that he already knows about the holiday. He says that he was offered the holiday first but couldn't take it 'due to pressure at work'. BUT, he's prepared to let you go instead. He has even spoken to some of your close family to look after your children. So there would be no challenge for you at all.

What would you do? What if this could really happen?

The company is also providing some spending money. You will have no personal expense. Think about it, two weeks in the sun, could you make it? I'm sure a few of you could be there. Now let's think forward to your holiday, let your imagination run. Can you picture walking along the shore, sand between your toes, the warm breeze coming off the blue sea, a beautiful clear sky, smell the tropical flowers in the background?

If you can imagine that clearly, maybe you could make the effort to take the trip. Suddenly you have to think about and write a list of all the things you need to do before you leave.

Let's say you to agree to take the holiday. What do you do next? The first thing might be to work out how long you have to get ready. You write a list of things to do, with some urgency. Suddenly you become more efficient and pick up the pace a bit. Who will feed the dog, who will write a note to cancel the milk while you are away? You start thinking and you start raising your tempo. Suddenly things get done a lot more quickly. You're even prepared to work through the night to get things ready. You would probably complete more things in that evening than you would do in a normal week. Why? Because now you have a reason, a goal to aim for, you have a new sense of purpose. You are excited.

In any case you would do that for a two-week holiday. But so many people don't do that for their lifestyle, or their future. They say: "I'll do it tomorrow." Then it doesn't get done. How many times have you thought about doing something and then forgotten to do it at the time. You remembered when it was too late.

There are times when your dream is so big that the facts don't count.

Making a 'To Do' list will make you 40% more effective.

It may seem uncomfortable to start with, maybe even difficult. With practice it will become a habit. This is about a daily routine of making lists of things that we need to do and when they need to be done, not just for a holiday. Think about it. If the reward is worth it you will be prepared to do it. Making 'to do' lists and planning the day is a daily routine that will enable you to be more effective and, therefore, more successful.

It is generally accepted that by reviewing your list at the end of the day and preparing one for the following day you will be up to 40% more effective. A review at the end of the day of what you achieved is very satisfying, especially when you can tick off the completed tasks. It is even more satisfying when you have completed those jobs you disliked but knew they had to be done.

You may know people who struggle to get to work in the mornings during the week and always seem to be late. Yet on a Saturday morning they get up at 5.00 a.m., go to the golf course or fishing by 6:30 a.m. It's because they make time and energy for the things they like doing. To be successful, we have to be disciplined to do things when they need to be done. It makes our daily routine really simple. In my observation, successful people are very disciplined.

Imagine that your mind is like a wardrobe and it's full. Your partner thinks you shouldn't go shopping for any more clothes because that wardrobe is too full. What's the solution? One solution, might be to separate things you haven't worn for the last twelve months. Box them up and send them to a charity shop. Obviously you don't need them otherwise you would have worn them in the last year. Perhaps half of your wardrobe hasn't been worn, maybe even more. The exciting thing is that, if you do it today, you can make space for new clothes, new goals.

If you think of that as your mind, decide to dump a lot of unimportant memories you hang on to, particularly negative events which happened in the past. This is baggage that is unhelpful and you don't need it. Just clearing your mind of all that negative history will help you to think more effectively, be more alert and focus on the things you can and should do.

When you think about it, you will find that most things in life that we worry about, aren't really so important after all. If you just focus on the major things, the minor things will take care of themselves.

For example: Ancient wisdom advises that you should build your business before you build your home and that you should dig a well before you are thirsty. Another proverb tells us that a good man leaves an inheritance for his children's children. That means cash not coupons.

Recently, my younger son, Joshua, came home from school with an ear-to-ear grin. "What are you smiling at?" I asked him. With a chuckle he replied: "Dad, I've just found out what inheritance means!" Later I was talking with my eldest son, Luke, he said to me: "Well dad if I don't have any children where would their money go?" Makes you wonder! Youngsters are smart these days aren't they? It doesn't seem all that long ago when I was a youngster living at home with my parents.

I remember a time, as I developed my business, when it seemed right to relocate. I saw a house out in the country near Devizes. It had a swimming pool, seven acres of land, outbuildings, and all the bathrooms I needed. What more could I want? That was until after we moved in and discovered the amount of work that was needed to renovate the house. The roof needed complete replacement. The outbuildings needed a lot of work to make them usable. We had the drive and front garden landscaped. It took me five years to redevelop the property during which time I was not developing my business as I should have done. My time was spent arranging builders, planning applications and all the sorts of extraneous tasks that were nothing to do with my work and really didn't interest me. I had become complacent. My life was freewheeling with no direction. I had let slip any sense of daily routine in my life.

Outwardly I had all the trappings of success but I had no time to enjoy my life and my family. My quality of life was really quite low. I had full time staff to deal with; builders needed decisions from me. I did not have a structured daily routine. I went from one crisis to another. In retrospect the work on the house had taken over my life. I was not resetting my goals.

Since this major distraction, I now live in a modern house which needs little or no maintenance. I have quality time; I take my boys to and from school, and I go to the gym during the day when it is quiet. I am able to attend all the school functions and sporting events. I am now in control of my time. Outwardly, I may appear less successful, inwardly I have fallen in love with myself again, because I have quality time for myself and my boys and I control my daily routine. I am able to get more things done each day because I plan my different activities in advance.

If you don't control your time somebody else will.

The Complacent Frog

A frog was put into a pot filled with cold water. The water was slowly heated. To start with the frog just accepted his circumstances and thought well this is simple; let's make the most of every situation. So he started doing some breaststroke, backstroke, swimming as happy as could be.

The owner turned the heat up a little bit more. The frog thought this was going to be a nice warm bath so he started bathing himself and really relaxing. Then the heat was turned up a little more. The frog thought to himself: "maybe it's a spa-bath I'm going to enjoy the benefits of this. They are really kind people."

Minutes later he was cooked.

The story of the frog sounds crazy. But there are people like this nowadays. Their circumstances at work are changing, they are working longer, and two jobs are being combined for one person to do. They are not sure where they are progressing. In many jobs there are fewer incentives, annual bonuses are no longer being paid and they are justifying their position to themselves as well as to others.

Maybe people need a big enough shock to get them to do something about their situations.

The Eaglet

High on a mountain, an eagle sat on her eggs. One of the eggs dislodged away from the nest and slowly little by little, as time went by, it gradually rolled down the mountain side. It continued until it arrived at the bottom, where there was a flock of prairie chickens pecking in the dust (you know prairie chickens; they flutter a bit and flap in the dust). One prairie chicken saw the egg and she pulled it into her nest with the rest of her eggs and she hatched it. A little eaglet emerged from the egg, just like the little prairie chicks hatched too.

One day the little eaglet looked up into the sky and saw an enormous bird gliding through the air with hardly any effort at all. The little eaglet said to himself: "Gee I wonder what kind of bird that is; I wish I could fly like that." The little eaglet started flapping in the dust with the other prairie chickens. He grew a little older and another day he looked up in the sky and saw an enormous bird again and said: "Gee I wish I could fly like that, I wonder what kind of bird that is." Then he forgot about it and went back to flapping in the dust and playing with the prairie chickens. In time the eaglet grew old, he looked up, saw the bird again and said: "I wonder what kind of bird that is. I wish I could fly like that."

Then the eagle died never knowing that he was an eagle; that he could fly high in the sky.

Too many of us live unfulfilled lives like that of the chicken when really we were born to soar above like eagles.

Key lesson

Know what you want and never give up. Reset your goals to new, higher ones.

1   *Do I know what I want?*

2   *Can I visualise it?*

3   *Do I really believe I can achieve it?*

4   *Do I have a mentor or coach to help me?*

5   *Have I established a routine to achieve it?*

6   *Do I write a list of tasks I need to do each day?*

7   *Do I review my list and routine every day?*

8   *In how many areas of my life am I doing these things?*

9   *Who controls my time?*

10   *What is my next goal after I complete this one?*

 ## WHAT I HAVE LEARNT TODAY

EVALUATE

Day 7

Evaluate - Summary

"Happiness is a by-product of achievement."   **E.C.McKenzie**

"Choice, not chance, determines destiny."   **E.C.McKenzie**

Today the word is to EVALUATE. Think about the value to you of your thoughts, your actions and where you are going. Evaluate your life; know your life values. It is with these that you make your choices.

To summarise, the 10 areas below have been important to help many people get started and moving forward. They are in no specific order. Remember your success is hidden in your daily routine:

1.   **REVIEW** your day and read out loud to yourself your goals and dreams twice daily - when you get up in the morning and when you go to bed at night. Doing this one activity alone puts you with the top earners in the country.

2.   **WRITE A 'TO DO' LIST** to help you to be more efficient in your work. Do it the night before. Jot down some actions you need to do. Statistics show that you will be 40% more efficient just by doing this. Keep focused on

97

each task and try not to start the next task until the current one has been completed. If you first do the activity on your list that you least like, then everything else will be easy.

3. **SHOW APPRECIATION** – people matter to you and you matter to them; give thanks with a grateful heart. Set yourself a goal that when you leave people they feel better about themselves than they did before. It's very rewarding. You will make their day better; it has a knock-on effect. Get used to giving people compliments; make them feel better. You will be rewarded with many new friends. Make it part of your daily routine.

4. **EXERCISE REGULARLY** not just once in a while. With a healthy body you can have a healthy mind. The exercise you do must be enjoyable to you, otherwise it becomes drudgery and you will drop it when something more interesting comes along. As with everything you must know your reason for doing it. There are countless people who join fitness clubs in January to shed the Christmas weight. They fall away by February or March because their reason is not big enough.

5. **TAKE NUTRITIONAL SUPPLEMENTS.** Why would you want to do that? Well, we already know that a factor in many major diseases is malnutrition in one form or another. It goes without saying that when you increase your exercise routine; you need extra nutrition and water. With more energy you can do more activities.

6. **SELF-DEVELOPMENT.** You do this by reading positive mental attitude books and attending training meetings and conferences on your subject. Spend time with successful people. That is a great place to start. It will stretch your horizons.

7. **LISTEN** to your mentor and act on the advice. Also listen to self-help CDs and tapes daily. Maybe you can do it when you're ironing, jogging, in your car on the way to work, dropping the kids off to school, even having a bath. There's a lot of time when you can listen. It doesn't have to take up prime-time. This will inspire you, and beats TV.

8. **ASSOCIATION.** Be aware of the people you associate with; particularly those who are on the journey that you want to be on. This is so important because you want to think and act the way they do. Consider carefully who you spend your time with.

9. **PLAN YOUR WORK** and work your plan towards your dreams, those goals you want to achieve. Consider the actions you need to do achieve them. When you're on the journey remember that planning is essential. If you plan correctly and do the right work at the right time, you can really move on. So don't put it off, don't procrastinate.

Those who fail to plan, in effect, plan to fail.

10. **QUALITY TIME** with your family. As part of my daily routine I make sure that I spend with my two sons. We take time out just to talk and listen together. We have found that this works for us at the end of the day over an early evening meal. The TV, computer and mobile phones are switched off so we have no distractions. The boys can tell me about their day, what they have done at school, what they are thinking.

If you've read this far you know my passion for cricket. You can imagine my pleasure in encouraging Luke and Josh since their selection for a county youth team. In evaluating my life and passions I can say that some of my proudest moment s have come with my children; especially when I have the opportunity to help them evaluate their own lives.

Recently, at age fourteen Luke was appointed Captain of the Under 15's. Also, you can imagine how pleased I was when Josh succeeded in his audition to be in "*Macbeth*" with the Royal Shakespeare Company.

Josh's RSC contract was at the same time as our Caribbean holiday to the cricket World Cup. He chose to stay in England for rehearsals and to practise for his own cricket matches. To me his dedication and commitment was that of someone with many more years of life and experience.

My children have been a constant reminder of what is possible and what can be obtained with "successful thinking". I can see in my boys great possibilities for their future as they associate with people who can genuinely nurture and guide them in their chosen careers.

The Philosopher and the Boy

The Greek philosopher Socrates was a wise man and very clever. One day a boy asked him: *"Will you teach me what it takes to be clever, intelligent, have knowledge, wisdom and experience like you have?"*

Socrates replied: *"Let's go down to the river."* So they went to the river together and the boy was very enthusiastic. Socrates took him into the river until they reached waist high. Socrates then put his hands on the boy's shoulders and pushed him down below the water level. The boy looked around for a while as he was looking for the secret of success. He saw a few fish and thought to himself: *"I wonder why I'm here."* A few seconds later he thought: *"I'm going to need some air."* So he started to push up gently. Socrates solidly held the boy down in the water. The boy pushed up a bit harder and thought to himself that Socrates might not realise that he needs to come up. So he pushed really hard; with all his power and strength and he was still under water. By then, with his last gasp of energy before the boy drowned, he pushed up, exploded and he left the water. Coughing, gasping and panting, he said to the wise man: *"What did you do that for? I came down to the river to find out how to be successful and you nearly drowned me."*

Socrates replied: *"Young man, remember that last gasp of air that you took? When you want success as much as you wanted that last gasp of air, that's what it takes to be successful. You've got to want to do it with every single ounce of your energy."*

This book isn't intended to 'drown' you. It will not push you into areas that you do not want to go but remember that just beyond your fear lies your success. My hope is that, with a few principles and guidelines to use in your own life, you create your own success through your daily routine. You can fly with the eagles. It's your choice.

YOUR SUCCESS IS:
HIDDEN IN YOUR DAILY -

Review

Opportunity

Use goals

Time with mentor

Ivestigate

Never, never give up

Evaluate

As you develop your daily routine you can have positive answers to the following questions:

1   *Am I grateful for what others do for me?*

2   *Do I set personal goals and recall them regularly?*

3   *Am I working towards my goals?*

4   *Do I have a regular exercise routine?*

5   *Do I watch what I eat?*

6   *Where do vitamins and nutrients fit in my food intake?*

7   *Do I write 'to do' lists?*

8   *Do I read self development books?*

9   *Do I listen to self help CDs and tapes?*

10   *Do I associate with like-minded people?*

11   *Do I spend quality time with my family?*

12   *Did this week or book exceed or fail to meet my expectations?*

 # WHAT I HAVE LEARNT TODAY

APPENDIX A

SEVEN DAY PLAN TO CLIMB YOUR MOUNTAIN

The enclosed guidelines could give you some ideas on how to create your own 7 day plan. Each day you work towards a better understanding of ROUTINE. For best results review goals and "live" your dreams at least twice daily.

Day 1 a.m.   **Review** TO DO list and your dreams.
                  Repeat each morning. Plan time to read each day.
      p.m.   Review your activities through the day.
                  Write TO DO list. Repeat each evening.

Day 2 a.m   Morning review as for day 1. When to read?
                  Think what **Opportunities** lie ahead today.
      p.m.   Evening review as for day 1.

Day 3 a.m   Morning review. When to read?
                  Use goals. Am I achieving the goals I set myself?
      p.m.   Evening review. Reading time?

Day 4 a.m   Morning review.
                  Time with Mentor Who can I contact today?
      p.m.   Evening review. Reading time?

Day 5 a.m   Morning review.
                  Investigate- How have I or could have improved my actions or results so far?

Day 6 a.m   Morning review. I'm committed to my routine.
                  I'll **never give up**.
      p.m.   Evening review. Reading time?

Day 7 a.m   Morning review. **Evaluate** my progress so far.
      p.m.   Evening review. Reading time?

APPENDIX B

RECOMMENDED READING

The following books and authors have helped me in my life and work.

The Bible

As a Man Thinketh	James Allen
Cash Flow Quadrant	Robert Kiyosaki
Eat That Frog	Brian Tracy
How Safe is Your Home?	Michael Fraser
How to Win Friends and Influence People	Dale Carnegie
Positive Personality Profiles	Dr Robert Rohm
Positive Power	Richard Taylor
Questions are the Answers	Allan Pease
Shape Shifter	Geoff Thompson
The Parable of the Pipeline	Burke Hedges
The Secret	Rhonda Bryne
To Dream or not to Dream	Dr Peter & Eva Müller-Meerkatz
Who Moved my Cheese?	Spencer Johnson
You Inc.	Burke Hedges

Turbo-charge your performance

in our workshops:

Your Success Is:
Hidden in Your Daily Routine

We offer workshops to enable you

to

Discover

Your Own Behaviour Responses

Experience

Personal Communication in Action

Apply

To Your Personal Daily Routine

The workshops are positive, simple and adapted to your individual needs.

The results are encouraging, effective and applicable in your daily life and work.

Visit us at: www.globaltraining4u.com